DON DESIGN

PERFECT PRESENTATION
ILLUSTRATION + PERSPECTIVE

オーバーレイフィルムの展開

水戸岡 鋭治 著

O. Burrell

EIJI MITOOKA & DON DESIGN ASSOCIATES

PERFECT PRESENTATION

ILLUSTRATION+PERSPECTIVE IN PANTONE® COLORS

Copyright © 1987
All rights reserved. No part of this publica-
tion may be reproduced or used in any form
or by any means——graphic, electronic, or
mechanical, including photocopying,
recording, taping, or information storage
and retrieval systems——without written
permisson of the publisher.

First Edition Sept. 1987
ISBN4-7661-0435-8

Graphic-sha Publishing Company Ltd.
1-9-12 Kudan-kita Chiyoda-ku Tokyo 102,
Japan
Phone 03-263-4318
Fax. 03-263-5297
Telex. J29877 Graphic
Printed in Japan

DON DESIGN

CONTENTS

■■■■■■■■■■■■

序

透明な光。爽やかな風。小鳥のさえずり。輝く海。そんな誰もが住んでみたい環境に、水戸岡さんの世界はある。そしてそこに描かれた暮らしはシンプルでアクティブ。人々があくまでも主体的にモノを選び、選ばれたモノたちは意味を語り掛ける。

そんなライフスタイルは, 水戸岡さんとドーンデザイン研究所のスタッフが理想に描く生活である。そのクリスプで明快な作風と相まって、この一連の魅力的な作品は観る人の眼を釘付けにし、気持ちを引きずり込んで止まない。

本編はカラーフィルムを駆使した最新技法を紹介する、イラストレーションの技術書と位置付けられている。『職人』を自認される水戸岡さんが開発された新しいテクニックがぎっしりと盛り込まれており、プロ、あるいはプロを志向する若い人たちにとっては格好のテキストとなろう。

しかし私にとって、本書はそれ以上の意味を持つ。既に刊行されている前二作と異なり、ここに紹介された多くの作品には、我々、都市生活者に対する提案が数多く織り込まれている。我々を複雑な現実から解き放たんとする夢が語られている。

そんな水戸岡さんの姿勢に、私は共感を覚えないではいられない。イラストレーションが世に与えうる影響力。即ち、作者の意図をものの見事に表現するデザインプレゼンテーションとして、今後のイラストレーションの在り方に大きな可能性を示唆しているように思えてならない。

『AXIS』発行人 石橋 寛

■

FORWARD

Birds singing in the warm sunlight. A gentle breeze caressing the sparkling ocean. It is this world that everyone dreams of that is home to the work of Eiji Mitooka. A life that is at once simple and active. The people in this world select the objects that surround them with loving care, and the objects exchange secret dialogues among themselves.

This is an ideal life conceived and depicted by Mitooka and his staff at Don Design Associates. The works presented here are representative of the mesmerizing power and crisp, clear tone that all of Mitooka's work possesses. Technically, this volume introduces a sampling of innovative overlay film techniques in illustration developed by Mitooka, and is sure to become a lasting reference for both professionals and students alike.

To me, however, this book has further significance. This work is different from his two previous publications in that he incorporates ideas that are especially meaningful to city dwellers in the illustrations presented here, ideas that are aimed at releasing us from the complicated reality of modern urban life. For this reason I feel a great empathy for his creative attitudes. His approach, a design presentation that conveys the designers aims and ideas perfectly, holds great possibilities for future illustration work, and its influence is destined to be felt throughout the world.

Publisher, Axis Hiroshi Ishibashi

DON DESIGN

はじめに
「マイナス」のための「パーフェクト」

あらゆる仕事で分業化が進むなかで、いくつものプロセスにさまざまな人々が関与するようになった。そこで必要となったのは、誰もが了解できる「ことば」なり「記号」である。ことに、仕事の成否が最終的に不特定多数の選択によって決まる場合は、そのことばや記号は「関係者」以外にも難なく通じる普遍性をもたねばならない。「プレゼンテーション」という作業は、そうした共通語の一つとして生まれた。出来上がるはずのものを予測し、表現し、とりあえずの合意に達するための拠りどころである。現在のプレゼンテーションに似た行為は、作る人と受けとる人、売る人と買う人との一対一の関係が成立した時点、すなわち物流が始まったはるか昔から存在したことだろう。

しかし今では、一人でなく数十、数百という人の目がチェックポイントにならび、それらを全てクリアしなければ取り引きも計画も進捗しない。フルイの目はおそろしく細かくなった。プレゼンテーションは厳密さと首尾一貫性に加えて、言語コミュニケーションにおける雄弁術のごとく、人を酔わせる力さえ備えなければならなくなった。

すでにこのシリーズの既刊書で述べたとおり、私はものごとを考え出した人が、どんな形にせよ自分でプレゼンテーションするのが本来の形と思っている。企画段階から仕事に参加する機会が与えられるようになった今、私は当然自分の手でそれを行っているが、幸か不幸か、絵が私の考えを伝える一番確実で楽な方法だからでもある。言葉は拙くて、思うこととの乖離ばかりを際立たせる。視覚に訴える伝達法は子供にもわかりやすいが、私にとって「ビジュアル・コミュニケーション」は決して第三者を意識した手段であるだけでなく、自分のなかにモヤモヤと発生してくるとりとめのない思いを整理してくれる思考の回路であり、それを表現してくれる「ことば」でもある。

私が絵によってプレゼンテーションするものは、「あるべき」とは言わないまでも「あってほしい」理想であり、それゆえ大マジメな絵空事である。

現実の目標が、「非現実的」の一言で退けられる理念を建前として組み立てられているように、プロジェクト実現の過程は、プレゼンテーション上の絵空事から一つ一つ、かけがえのない要素をマイナスしてゆく作業の積み重ねに他ならない。タイトル中の「PERFECT」はそのことを指す。これは「完璧に上手なプレゼンテーション」を教える本ではなく、クライアントと私と私の仲間たちが夢と希望と丹精をこめて描き、そして間もなく、ある種の諦めや、かけひきや制約によって現実味を帯びてくる、ドリームプランの集合なのである。

7年目の「オーバーレイ」

今から7年前に「イラストレーション＋パースペクティヴ」シリーズの1冊目を出したとき、その主な画材はロットリングとカラーインクだった。その頃は、画面中央にボヤンとした筆使いで、くすんだ色の巨大な建物が屹立する絵がパースの代表のようだったが、私は、単に「クッキリ・ハッキリ」が好きだという理由でペンとインクを選び、せっせと自分の手を動かして描いていた。余談だが、当時、我がドーンデザインは木造モルタルアパートの一室にあり、亡くなられた前川國男先生がパースの捗り具合を見に(?)わざわざ訪ねてこられたときは、とにかくバツが悪くて困った。お付きの人に支えられるようにしてアパートの外階段

を昇ってこられた先生は、私が万年床としていたクタビレたソファにチョコンと座られて、莞爾としておられた。悠揚として迫らぬ風韻で発せられた「そう、よくかけてるね」の一言と、手持ち無沙汰のあまり、故郷から届いたばかりの岡山名物『大手まんじゅう』をお出ししたことだけを、今でもよく覚えている。件の熊本県民ホールのコンペは、めでたくも先生が勝たれて、本当に嬉しかった。

それからしばらくして、キトクにも弟子入り志願者が現れたため、師匠としては、経験や技術の差があまり目立たない制作方法を考えざるを得なくなった。そこで、個性や技量がモロに出る筆に代えてエアブラシの均質的な「塗装面」を採用したところ、「品質」のバラツキはかなり抑えられるようになり、同時に、マスキングフィルムのカットという新しい「職種」が生まれた。ウチの「社史」年表で言うと、このシリーズの「エアブラシ」編の刊行、さらには木造アパートから鉄筋コンクリートの一室への「社屋移転」という快挙が成し遂げられた時代に重なる。そして「ペン&インク」から7年目にして、今回の「オーバーレイ」の登場である。エアブラシ時代に培われた、気の遠くなるようなフィルムカッティングの技術を前面に押し出し、「切って貼る」という二つのプロセスで作品の大半を仕上げてしまう大胆な「合理化」に踏み出したのである。防塵マスクとエプロンといういでたちで臨むエアブラシングを、色作りの時点だけを残して大幅に減らすことによって、「低公害」の職場も実現できた。

「切り貼り」だけを取りだせば、これはもう素人にもすぐ取りかかれる仕事である。「雇用の創出」に見事に応えることができる。だれにでもできるといっても、決して卑下するには及ばず、習うのに要するエネルギーを完成度を上げるほうに振り向けてもらうだけの違いである。いろいろな人たちが寄ってたかって揉みあげるようにして一つの作品を創り出す。それがウチのシステムであり、費やされる時間と労力の上澄みだけを掬い取った、その密度の濃さが生命だと思っている。イラストレーションは「商品」なのだから、一定時間内に仕上がらなくては意味がない。一人ではとうてい追いつかない私は、誰でも「即戦力」となるしくみをいつも考えてきた。「立ってる者は親でも使え」という切迫した動機が、知らずしらず「全ての人に働く場所を」という気高い理想に転じた(?)のは、思ってもみなかった僥倖、ヒョウタンから駒の余録である。

しかし、一人分の負担を頭数に振り分けて「とりあえず皆で出来るところからやろうね」という姿勢は、いやしくも絵かきの道にモトる、厳しい自己実現の試練を放棄している、と言われるかもしれない。実際、仕事場の引越しというエポックごとに画法がコロコロ変わり、作品は「自己」に収斂するどころか、いよいよコルホーズ的体制、というか、「マニュファクチャリング」の域に入りつつある。「生産ラインの確立と品質管理」を専らとする私は、アートの世界の住人である前に、風にそよぐ「個人事業主」であるようだ。

ペン&インクからオーバーレイへの移行は、このマニュファクチャリング路線の強化に他ならない。しかし、7年目のオーバーレイはただの心変わりではなく、7年間の蓄積である。ペンもインクもエアブラシもオーバーレイも投入して出来上がった作品が、私たちにとって、よりクリエイティヴな領域を拓くための有効な手段となったことを感じとっていただければ、この本の目的は達せられたことになる。

DON DESIGN

デジタル昂じてアナログと化す

さて、オーバーレイによるイラストの生産ラインが整ったとする。不器用な私に残された仕事のなかで一番悩むのが色指定だが、この作業が格段にやりやすくなった。イラストレーションは印刷に付して初めて真価が問われるものだから、印刷された時点での色の出具合を予測しながら原画の色を指定しなければならない。カラーインクは確かに色の出はよいが、筆やエアブラシで一度画面に載ってしまうと、修正はほとんど絶望的である。それに較べ、貼り直しのできるオーバーレイは、シミュレーションが可能という一点を取っても実にありがたい。思いきった色構成ができる。冒険ができる。労力さえ厭わなければ、コンピュータの画像のように色の差し替えは、理論上いくらでも可能である。スタッフには大きな声で言えないが「人力グラフィックスクリーン」と呼んでもよいくらいである。ただ、オーバーレイの種類は豊富なので、最適の素材を選び、印刷上りの目安がつくまである程度時間がかかった。

近頃「デジタル」と「アナログ」という分類のしかたが盛んだが、フィルムの切り貼りが数量化されたデジタルとすれば、手の動き一つで決まる筆描きはアナログと言えよう。「無名」の微細な紙片を集めて画面を作ってゆく「フィルム画」に対し、描き手の息づかいやココロまで表出させる「筆画」は、前者にない「個性」や「人間的」なぬくもりを伝える、とさえ評される。けれど、本当にそうなのだろうか。デジタル作業を愚直といえるほど丁寧に積み重ねてゆけば、アナログの極致ともいえる手仕事の最高峰、すなわち筆による細密画にも対抗できる「質感」と「情感」が表現できるのではないだろうか。現に、一つ一つの構成要素は「カチッ」としていても、画面全体を見渡すと、色も香りもあり、しっとりと重みさえ含んだ空気が確かに流れているのではないだろうか。私の絵は遠く及ばないまでも、鈴木英人氏のイラストレーションを例に挙げれば、納得していただけることだろう。このデジタルからアナログへの「質的転換」は、私にとって一大発見だった。

それに、さらにもう一つアナログ・タッチを加えるなら、既製の色をオリジナル化する方法がある。エアブラシや筆で色をかけたり柄を載せることによって、オーバーレイはただのフィルムではなく、自分で調合した「絵具」と化し、カッターナイフが絵筆の代わりを務めることになる。自分の抱くイメージが、予想を越えた明晰さで鮮やかに浮かび上がってくることだろう。オーバーレイが、ひたすらわかりやすく、思いきりよく表現するしかないプレゼンテーションに最適の画材であることは、経験上間違いない。

時代の風向きが変わってきたおかげで、わずかずつ暖めてきたアイデアや夢物語を発表する番が私にも巡ってきた。しかしこの先何年かして、もしやまた「引越し」という事態になったとき、オーバーレイの次に来るのはコンピュータグラフィックスとの邂逅か、あるいは筆との再会か。いずれにせよ、地道で緻密な職人的マニュファクチャリングは変わらないことだろう。孫引きで恐縮だが、こんな話がある。ポール・ヴァレリーが、美術館に展示されたアンリ・ルソーの絵を見て「実に見事だが、あれだけの葉を一枚一枚描くのはさぞ面倒なことだっただろう」とドガに言ったとき、ドガは即座に「面倒でなければ面白くもなかっただろう」と答えたそうである。この言葉を玩味する資格があるのは、私ではなく、私の「アソシエイツ」である。

INTRODUCTION

This book is the third to be published in the series ⟨Illustration+Perspective⟩ since its inception seven years ago. The subject of the first volume was the use of pen and colored ink, the second volume concerned airbrushing techniques and this volume introduces the technique and applications of overlay film in rendering.

One of the best known overlay film is PANTONE color Letrafilm which is distributed by Letraset. Here I wish to acknowledge with gratitude Letraset Co., Ltd. as well as Letraset Japan Co.,Ltd., who have generously given their permission to use their product name ⟨PANTONE⟩ in the title of the overseas edition. I myself have found the variety of color and tone in this product to be invaluable in my field of work. However, due to the nature of my work I have sometimes also found it necessary to adapt the product, experimenting with a number of my own ideas and techniques.

In Japan, perspectives, known under the typical Japanese abbreviation "pers", have come to mean the architectural renderings used in the advertising activities of the construction industry, rather than the painting technique which developed remarkably in the Renaissance period. Such are the demands of the commercial world these days that even my style of rather exceptional "pers" has become accepted and has established its own position in commercial illustrations, exceeding its recognized function in architecture.

Since these architectural renderings illustrate an ideal and yet attainable near-future lifestyle, they have become a kind of "Ukiyoe" of present-day Japan. You will find, in these pages, another side of the high-technological reality in Japan, including recent trends of art, design and fashion, and the dream of ordinary people for housing, resorts and thier own lifestyles. The main role of the renderer is to describe a more prosperous lifestyle by the addition of imaginative foresight to a solid foundation of culture and tradition. For this reason the perspective representation is not simply a two-dimentional drawing technique, but has a definite role to play in the world of commercial graphic art.

Included in this book are many presentations of long-term projects, among them, resort developement projects. The use of perspectives in this type of planning is growing, and thus the role of perspective renderers has changed ; they are now being asked to do more than simply produce straight-forward renderings of architectural ideas and are using their own unique insight into the future. The use of overlay film enables the perspective renderer to transfer his ideas on to paper and its use will expand as his role expands. I believe the recognition of such a visual comunication as one of the most effective media means the acceptance of a "common language", which is readily understood by people throughout the world.

Because of this universal quality I dedicate this book not only to those who aspire to become architectural renderers but also to those who love architecture, illustration and life.

NEO ARCADIA

ネオ アルカディア

『オーチャードクラブ』『ヴィレッジクラブ』『アクアクラブ』という、それぞれ農・林・水産業を経済基盤とする地域を想定したリゾート建設案は、私がこれまでいくつかの誌上に発表してきたイラストとエッセイの断片や、無邪気な思いつきを掻き集めて出来上がった。いわば単なる「出来ごころ」である。

そもそもの発端は、北欧からドイツにかけて旅行中、車窓から市民菜園「クラインガルテン」とその園亭「ラウベン」を偶然「見てしまった」ことだった。日本の都市近郊農地は、観光地へ辿り着くまでの、決して美しいとは言えない車窓の風景にすぎない。無節操な商業化で荒廃した土地も多い。それを「クラインガルテン・コロニー」として開発し、宿泊・スポーツ施設を併設した会員制田園リゾートを建設しようというのが、『オーチャードクラブ』の主旨である。森林地帯と海辺に計画された他の二つのクラブも、同様の発想から、ほぼ自動的に生まれたヴァリエーションである。

いずれも、各地域の基幹産業を破壊することなく、地元の人々のイニシアティヴで運営されることを目指している。三つのクラブのうち二つはすでに実現に向けて調査段階に入っているが、経営収支上はともかく、地元の人々と来訪者とが本当に「平和的」に共存することができるものなのか、いくら楽観的な私でも容易に断言はできない。

東洋の「桃源郷」と同じように、西洋には古いギリシャの一地方を舞台にした理想郷「アルカディア」がある。これがウェルギリウスの詩作上の想像の産物でしかなかったように、私の「ネオ・アルカディア」が幻想に終わっても、創作上の「箱庭遊び」を私自身は十分堪能した。

The ORCHARD CLUB, VILLAGE CLUB and AQUA CLUB are three resort projects planned for areas whose main industries are respectively agriculture, forestry and marine products.

I started thinking about this kind of project while travelling in Germany where I saw 〈KLEINGARTEN–garden allotment〉 and 〈LAUBEN–cabin〉. On my return I decided to use the ideas I had conceived, coupled with visions of my own, to create a project for developing an area not normally considered for tourist resorts.

In Japan, agricultural land on city outskirts is the kind of landscape you see as a tourist through a train window on your way from the city to a resort area. This area is often rather unattractive and some have been ruined by unplanned commercial development. The ORCHARD CLUB was set up to develop an area of this "no man's land" as a "Kleingarten Colony", linked to hotels and sports facilities with a membership system. The project was planned around local industries employing local initiative in its construction and maintenance.

The VILLAGE CLUB and AQUA CLUB projects grew out of the same basic ideas, but were developed along different lines according to their location and economic activity. Two of these three resort concepts are already under consideration for production.

A peaceful co-exsistance between visitors and local people has been a problem since the dawn of civilization. For this reason I named these projects, after the Greek utopian country Arcadia, NEO ARCADIA.

■■■■■

農水林

農
ORCHARD CLUB

The ORCHARD CLUB
Symbol mark

water & earth

spring leaves

sun

水
AQUA CLUB

The AQUA CLUB
Symbol mark

waves

fish

sea

林
THE VILLAGE CLUB

The VILLAGE CLUB
Symbol mark

tree

wood

forest

私の『ネオ・アルカディア』を具現する三つの会員制リゾートクラブ構想に共通するのは、地元の生活圏の中に「混ぜてもらう」という姿勢と、人工的に自然を「造る」という企てである。

会員は囲み地のなかに隔離され、本来の住人は柵の外から眺めている、といった図だけは避けたい。会員の遊び場が、地元の生産の場・生活の場と隣り合わせになっていて、互いに暮らしを覗き見る・見られるというシゲキが大切なのである。また、自然であれば何でも美しいという意識は、ここにはない。水も緑もデザインの最も重要な対象である。『オーチャードクラブ』を例に取ろう。 ゾーニングは

■農場—地元の農業従事者による生産の場
■クラインガルテン—会員の専用区画やレクリエーションの場
■バーン—「納屋」すなわち管理・サービスの場

というように、素人が玄人の模範「演技」を間近に見ることができる。玄人が素人に指導することができる。栽培が苦手なら、自分の区画でひねもすウツラウツラしていたり、スポーツをしたり、ホテルでアフター5を楽しんでもよい。専用区画内には、ラウベンを模した縮小したスケールのミニハウスがあって、自分だけの休息所となる。三つのクラブに共通した空間構成要素は、この「専用区画とミニハウス」であって、日常生活丸ごと移動型の別荘地とも、ホテル生活とも根本的に異なる点である。

このような遊びと生産が同居するコミュニティーでは、CIから建物まで、あらゆるデザインがニュートラルであるほうがよい。「カントリースタイル」や「郷土色」をことさら強調するアクの強い演出は、必要ない。

その代わり、こころもち「カワイク」あればよい。大人が見たり使ったりするものについて、カワイらしさはむしろ排除すべき要素のように言われるが、私は、特にこうした遊び場では、はぎれの良さとか洗練度よりもカワイ気が大切であり、かつ長持ちすると思っている。

Mini-houses seen from the waterway/perspective

The three membership resort clubs, which are part of my concept of ⟨NEO ARCADIA⟩ have two principles in common ; a non-exclusive attitude towards the local residents, which allows for a harmonious relationship rather than typical combative one, and an attempt to artificially create a natural environment.

I was anxious that a future scene of members, isolated from the local residents by a wall, would never occur. If the two sides could integrate their daily lives, with the members' "playground" next door to the residents' work area, this unavoidable contact would produce a stimulating and beneficial experience. In addition, an aesthetic sense that indiscriminately adores all and any kind of "natural beauty", is, for me, not valid here. Although water and greenery will be the focal points of the design, the "natural" environment will have to be arranged and manipulated to fit our plans.

In case of the ORCHARD CLUB, the zoning of the site will be as follows :

■ ⟨FARM⟩ for local farmers
■ ⟨GARDEN ALLOTMENTS & RECREATION AREA⟩ for members

■ ⟨BARN⟩ as an administrative office and service center

Holiday "farmers" will be able to learn the techniques of cultivation from "professionals", or do sports and other activities such as participating in the night life available at the clubhouse and hotel.

Each allotment has its scaled-down ⟨mini-house⟩ which is modeled on the German ⟨Lauben⟩. This layout of space consisting of ⟨an allotment with its mini-house⟩ is repeated consciously throughout the other clubs, and provides the guests with a unique leisure life, whereby they can enjoy both the privacy of their individual retreats and participate in the social life of the various public facilities.

In such a comuity of play and production, it is advisable that the designs, from corporate identity to buildings, should be as neutral as possible, avoiding too emphasis on "coutry style" or "local color".

Instead, a touch of "charm" will be needed. It seems that charm has been eliminated consciously from the world of adults, but I think, especially in such a resort, it is more significant and lasts longer than "sophistication".

VISUAL IDENTITY

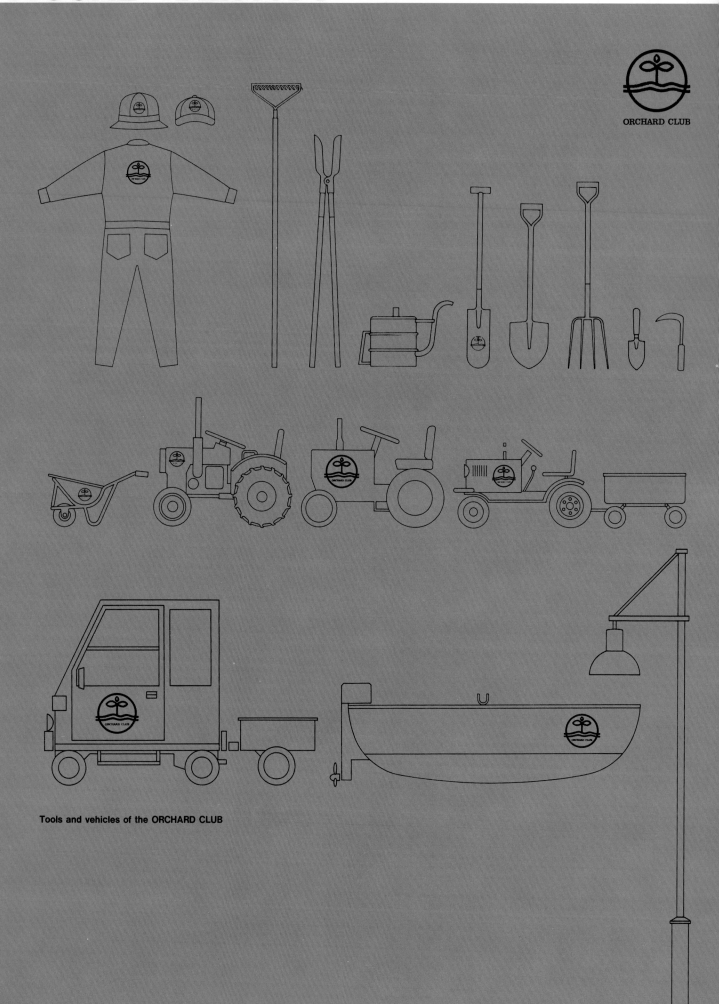

ORCHARD CLUB

Tools and vehicles of the ORCHARD CLUB

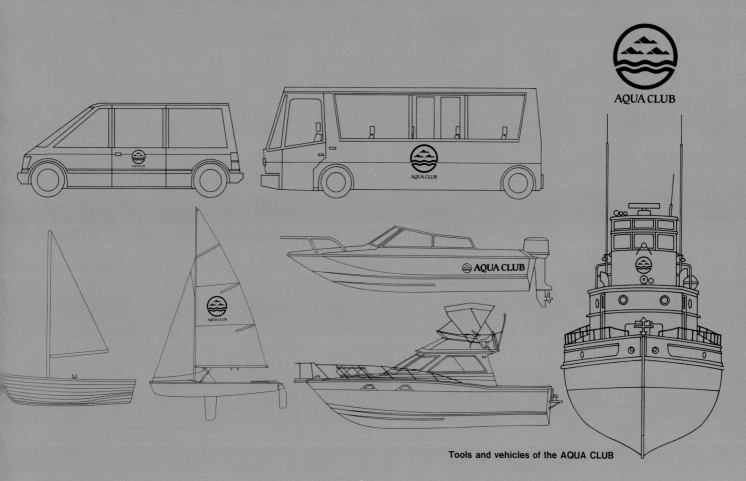

AQUA CLUB

Tools and vehicles of the AQUA CLUB

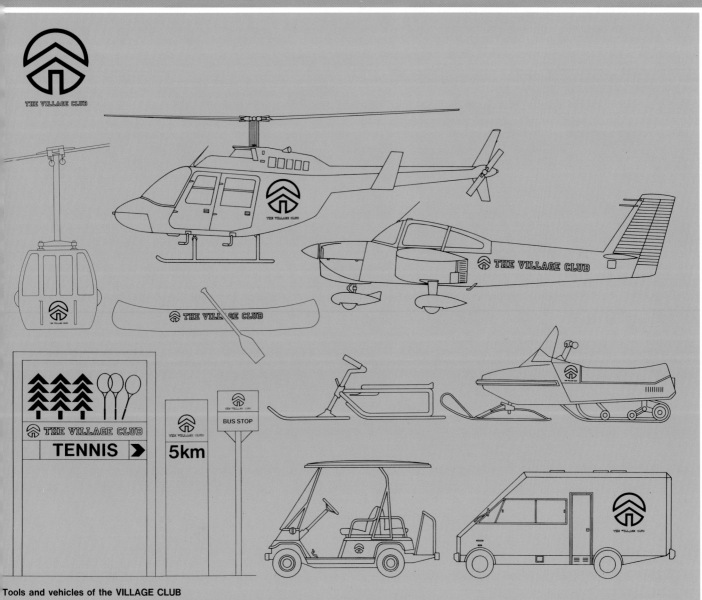

THE VILLAGE CLUB

TENNIS ▶

5km

BUS STOP

Tools and vehicles of the VILLAGE CLUB

ORCHARD CLUB

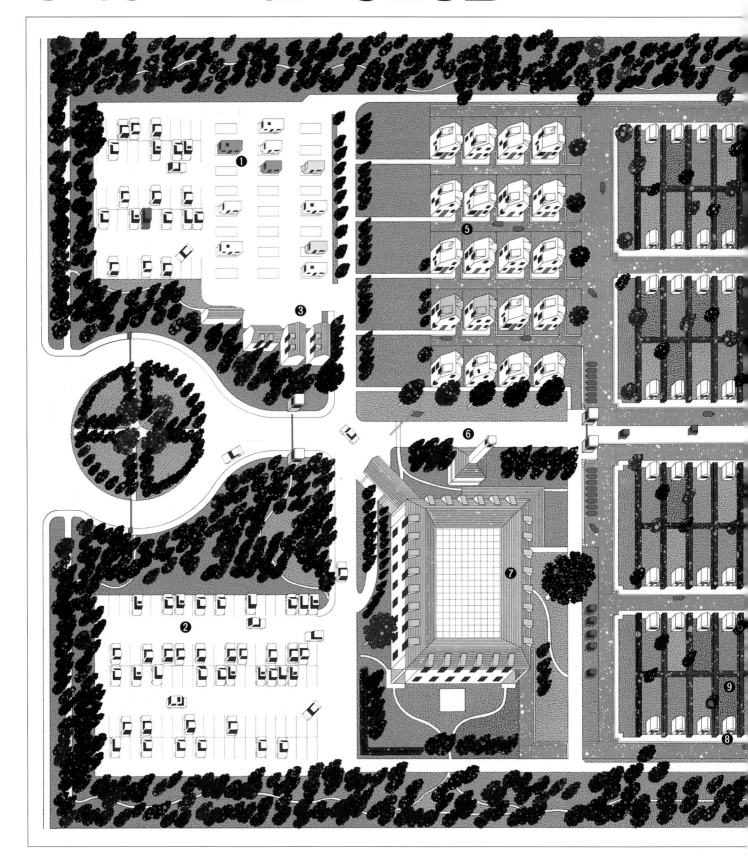

ORCHARD CLUB

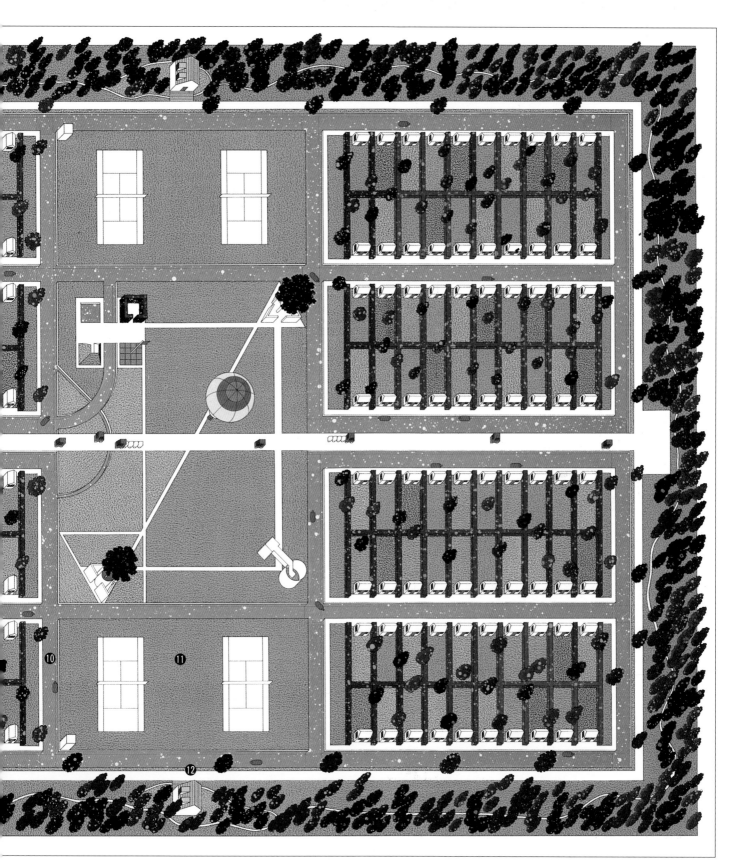

Site plan of the ORCHRAD CLUB
① Campers lot　　　　　　⑦ Hotel
② Parking lot　　　　　　　⑧ Mini-houses
③ Shops and bathrooms　　⑨ Garden allotments
④ Main gate　　　　　　　⑩ Waterway
⑤ Cottages　　　　　　　⑪ Tennis court
⑥ Administrative office　　⑫ Clubhouse

A

C

A Weekend scene in front of cot-
  tages/elevation
B Cottages seen from the water-
  way/perspective
C Garden allotments, mini-houses
  and waterway/section

ORCHARD CLUB

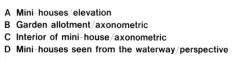

A Mini-houses/elevation
B Garden allotment/axonometric
C Interior of mini-house/axonometric
D Mini-houses seen from the waterway/perspective

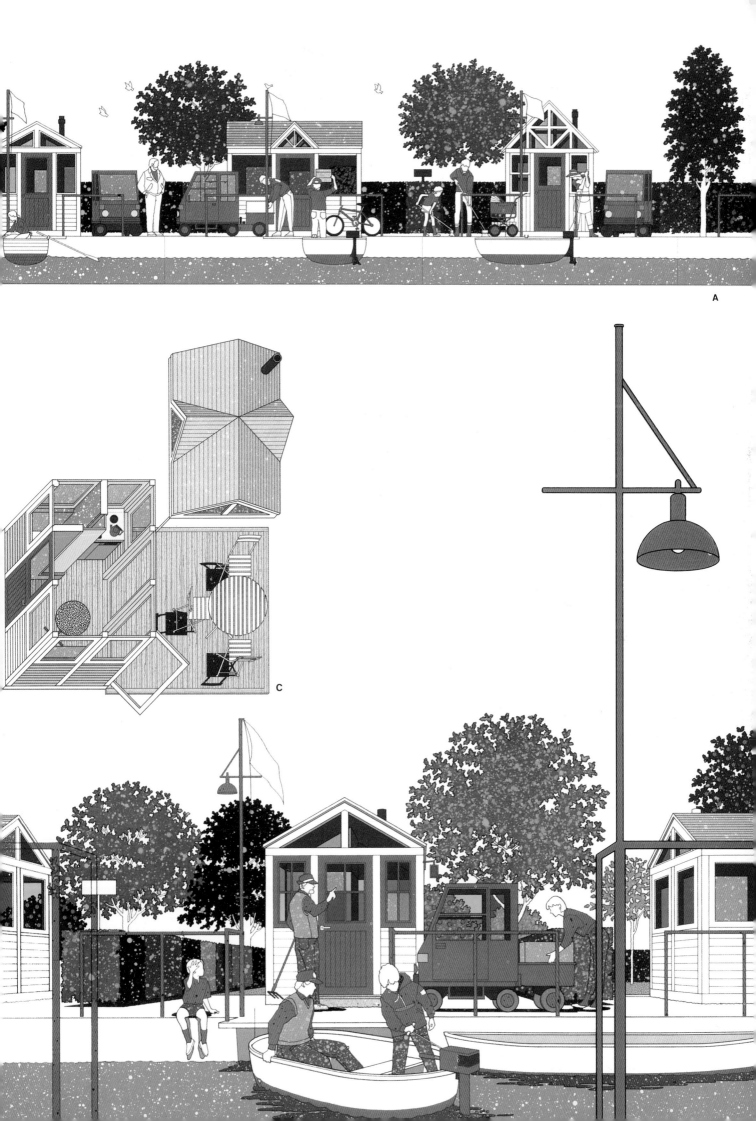

A

C

AQUA CLUB

『アクアクラブ』では三つのライフスタイルが共存する。海で働く漁師たち、ハウスボートに住む人々、そして、海辺の区画で週末を楽しみ、ホテルに滞在する人々の生活である。

マリンスポーツに熱中するだけが目的でなく、海の近くでただブラブラしたい人も溶けこめる環境や施設を造りたい。このプランを描いている間、私はちょっとした「港町」の縮小版を再現する気分だった。

In the AQUA CLUB there are three types of lifestyles coexisting; that of local fishermen, houseboat residents and those people who enjoy weekends in their seaside allotments, clubhouses and hotels.

I tried to create an environment and facilities not only for marine sports enthusiasts but also people who want to spend a relaxing time by the sea. While rendering this plan on to paper, I felt I was reproducing a small model of a lively port town.

Site plan of the AQUA CLUB
❶ Parking lot
❷ Administrative tower
❸ Shops
❹ Hotel
❺ Refit shop
❻ Sail loft
❼ Boatyard
❽ Yacht harbor
❾ Boathouse
❿ Tennis court
⓫ Restaurant
⓬ Market
⓭ Fishermen's houses
⓮ Clubhouse and shops
⓯ Cottages
⓰ Pool
⓱ Hotel
⓲ 〈Cruise in〉
⓳ Hotel
⓴ Cottages
㉑ Sandy beach
㉒ Boardwalk
㉓ Mini-houses
㉔ Restaurants

AQUA CLUB

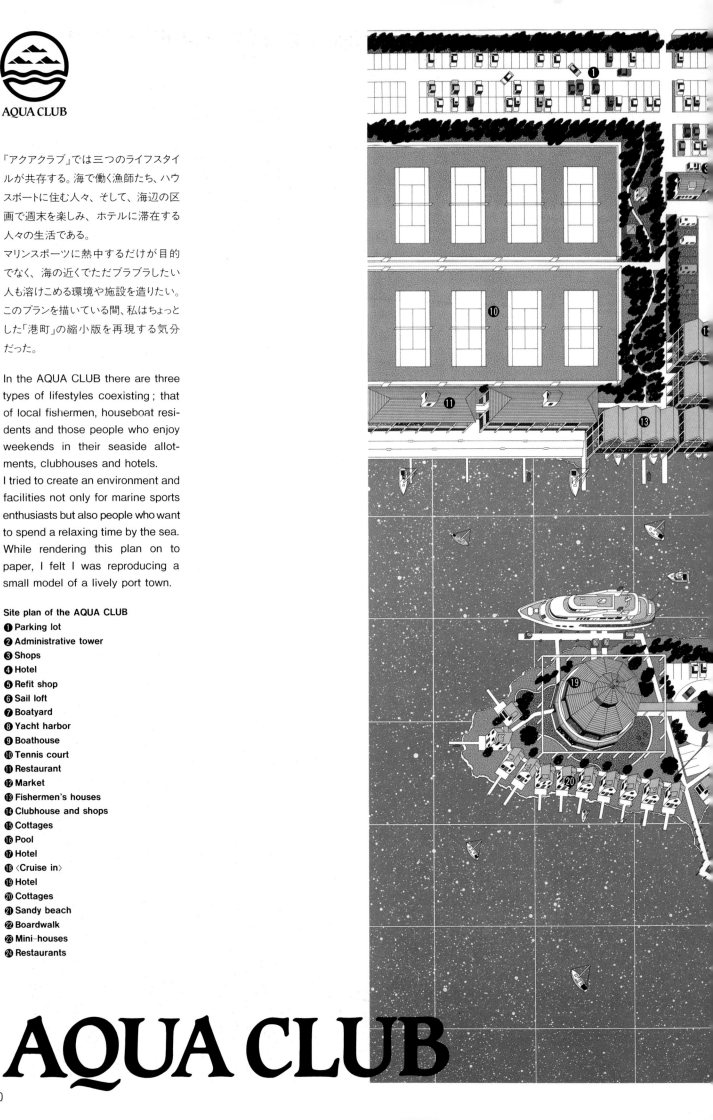

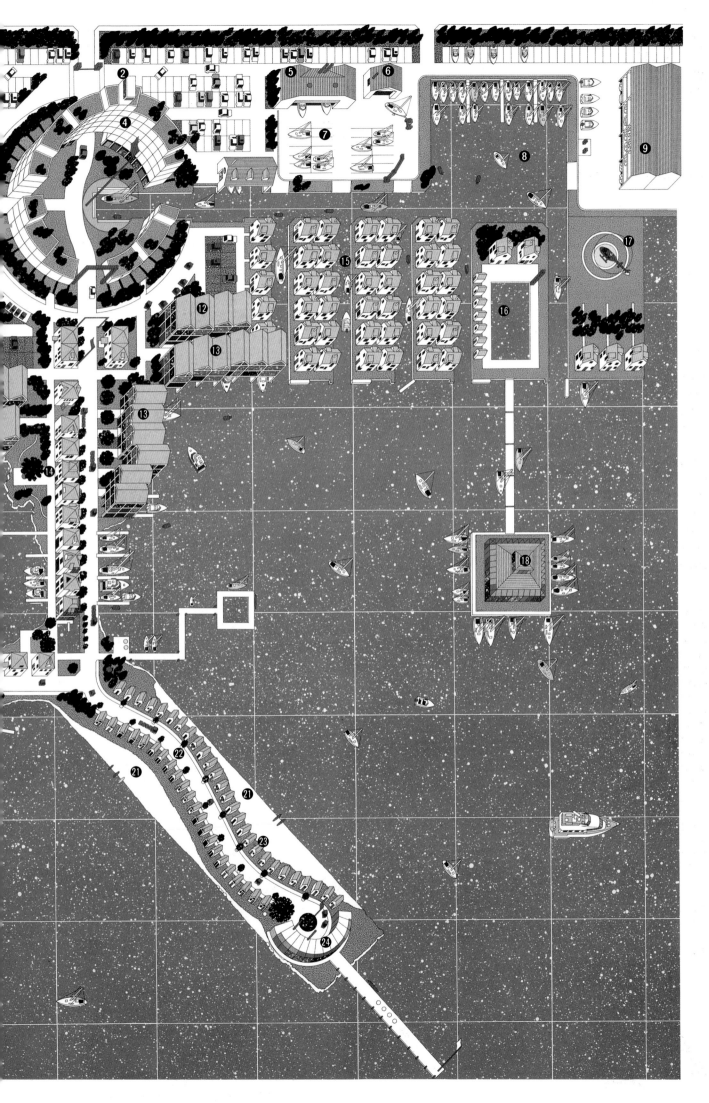

AQUA CLUB

P22-23 Marina/section of the site plan
P24-25 Landscapes with various types of cottages and pier/perspective

AQUA CLUB

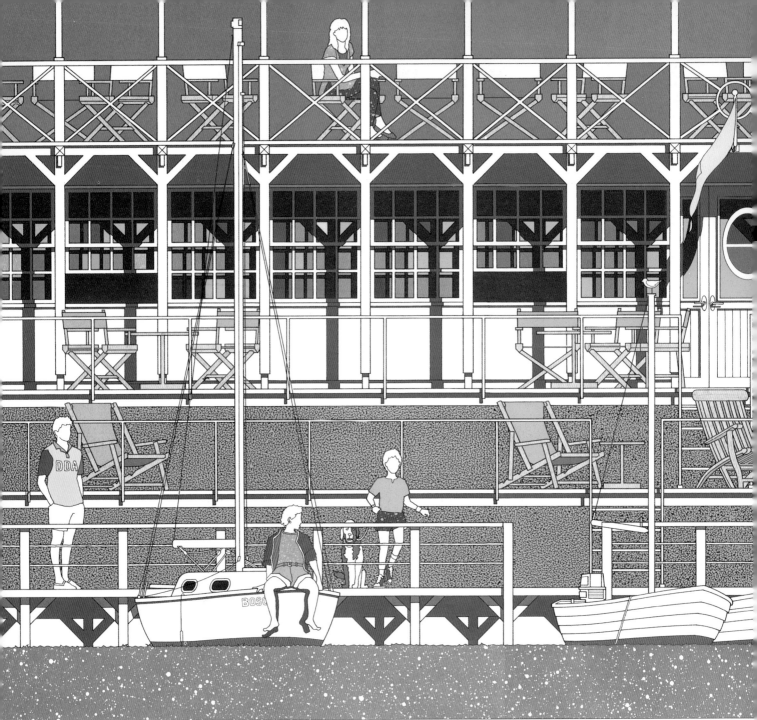

AQUA CLUB

A Seaside restaurant with 3 levels/elevation
B Floating rest house 〈CRUISE-IN〉/perspective
C Christmas dinner in seaside restaurant/perspective

A

C

B

A Interior of boathouse/
  perspective
B Boathouse/elevation
C Row of boathouses/
  elevation

C

AQUA CLUB

⟨ROPE FERRY⟩
that carries people and vehicles/perspective

B

C

A Marina/axonometic
B Pier seen from cottages/perspective
C Interior of houseboat/perspective

AQUA CLUB

AQUA CLUB

A

A Cottage in the woods
B Marina/elevation

B

34

HOTEL UMINONAKAMICHI

ホテル海の中道

『ホテルの海の中道』は『国営海の中道海浜公園』の一角に今年の春オープンした。海は目の前、福岡市内からも1時間という申し分ない環境にある。そんな理想的なリゾートホテルのアートディレクションという仕事も、考えてみれば、ここまで紙の上でやってきた「容れもの」と「容れられるひと」との間でウオウサオウする作業を実地に移すことなのだった。期待しうる最良の過ごし方と最高の舞台を提示するために、ホテルという「建物」と、スタッフおよびゲストという「人」との間に介在する、あらゆるモノの機能と形と色を決める、建物と人を結ぶ至近距離に道をつける仕事である。

具体的には、CIを作り、用具や備品やユニフォームをデザインしたり選択し、それらを配置し、イラストを描き、紙面やTV画面に載せるという「開店」までの雑役をこなすこと、あらゆるスキマをモノとアイデアで埋めつくすことだった。モノの少ない時代に育った私にとって、帰り来ぬ岡山での青春のアダを福岡で討つかのような「モノ尽くし」の仕事は、シンドイながらも楽しかった。

だが、ホテルは人が主役であり、モノを見せる場ではない。それぞれいっぱしのモノを集めながら、今度は全体の調和のなかで限りなく没個性に近づけ、「雰囲気」という無形のものに奉仕させなければならない。傑出したセンスより、今では懐かしい「趣味や品のよさ」のほうが「くつろぐ」という目的に一番似合うと思うのだが、日本のように特定の「クラス」ではなく、ある「年代」を、特に若者を意識した場合には、一見して「ちょっと違う」とアピールする「即戦力」が求められる。絵ではそのへんを勘案して、ハメをはずすくらいのヴィヴィッドな表現に徹した。

On the sea front, only an hour from the Fukuoka city center, the HOTEL UMINONAKAMICHI is in a perfect location for a resort hotel. I originally thought that my duty of creating a "perfect environment" as art director of this project, was an almost impossible task, yet I soon realized that my role was an extention of that of an illustrator ; combining imaginaion with a sense of reality, it was the practical application of paper work to a tangible existence.

In commencing a project of this nature, the primary consideration has to be the color, form and function of the hotel envitonment, which provide the link between humans and their surroundings. The ultimate aim of this work is to create an ideal "stage" for peole to enjoy themselves.

In this case it meant, producing corporate identity, selecting and positioning the furniture, lighting, stationary and other small articles, designing uniforms and drawing the illustration for TV and newspaper advertising as well as the many other odd jobs that are required in preparation for a hotel opening.

The leading role in this scene is played by people, so the materials should not intrude but should harmonize with the total environment. Although the project itself is rather conventional, with the object of comfort and relaxation the main intention, the advertising strategy aimed at attracting the younger generation has created an overall impression of youth and vitality.

Various human figures/poster, newspaper and other advertising

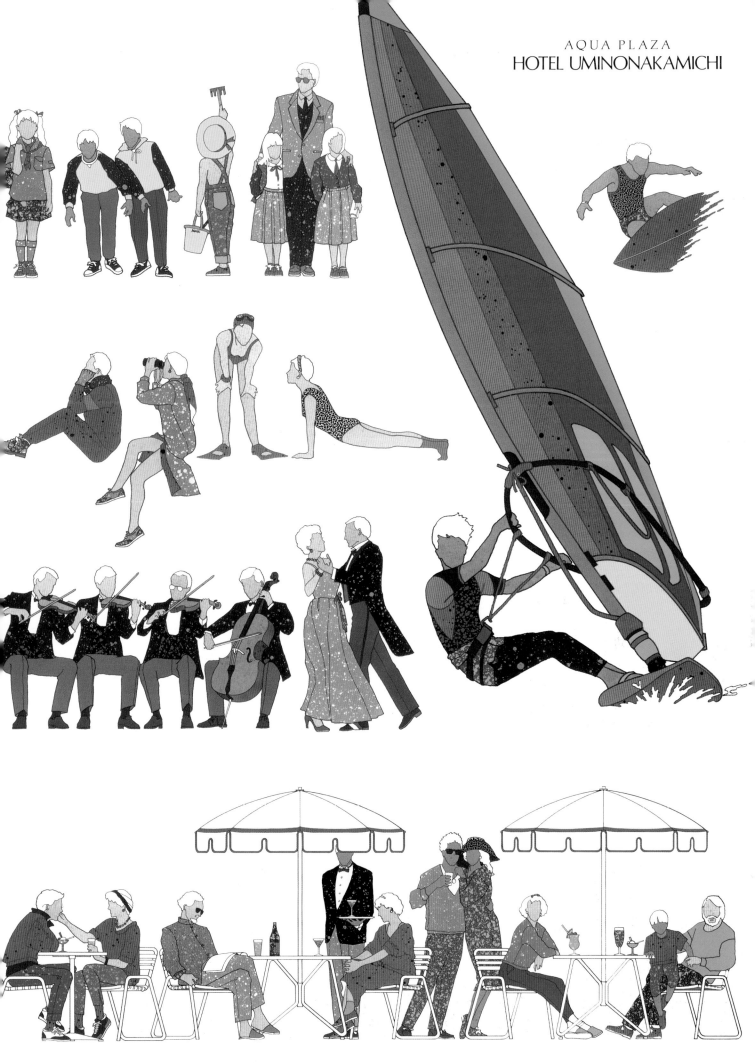

Various human figures

みずみずしい半島。

いま、「国営海の中道海浜公園」一帯では、ビッグなプロジェクトが進行中です。
540ヘクタールの広大な敷地。大自然に包まれたプレイグラウンド・海浜公園に、
この4月、いよいよ「ホテル海の中道」、マリーナ、そしてセミナーハウスがオープン。
さらに将来は、海洋生態科学館、アウトドアシアターなど、スポーツと
カルチャーを楽しむ多彩な施設が計画されています。
“公園”の枠をはるかに超えるこのエリア一帯を、
私たちは「AQUA RESORT(アクア・リゾート)」と呼びたいと思います。
人と水。人は水から生まれ、遊びは水から始まります。
かつて、豊かな水のほとりに人が集まり、そこからさまざまな素晴らしい文化が生まれたように、
この「AQUA」から、人と海と大地を結ぶ新しい文化が生まれることを願って。

AQUA

1987年4月25日OPEN

AQUA PLAZA

ホテル海の中道

海の中道海浜公園

B

C

AQUA PLAZA
HOTEL UMINONAKAMICHI

A Bird's-eye view of the hotel location/
  posters used for advertising at railway stations
B Bird's-eye view of the hotel location/
  poster, magazine and other advertising
C Elevation of pool-side scene/catalogue and
  newspaper advertising
D Perspective of the hotel/
  calendar, poster and catalogue

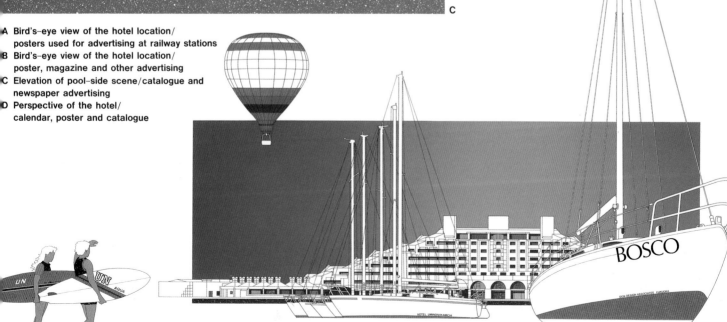

D

Stationary and other small items for the hotel

CASA PROJECT

カーサ プロジェクト

株式会社カーサプロジェクトがこの秋河口湖にオープンするモデルハウス、CASA MIA はこれまでにない企画・設計・施工システムを展開する。モデルハウスで丸一日「生活」を体験し、施主と設計者の対話を成立させるための共通の「言語」を探りだすところから始めるのである。設計室も置かれた広大な敷地に、展示される住宅は2棟。それらをイラストにした。

いつもと勝手が違うのは、純西欧型の住宅であることである。タタミの部屋は一つもない。「日本にも靴を脱がない住宅がついに来たか」と、一瞬どういう類の感情か名伏しがたいながら、ともかくも「感無量」ではあったが、間もなく抵抗はなくなった。究極の「洋」を知るためにはここまで行くしかない、「洋」の徹底が「和」の再評価にも役立つものと思えるようになった。さらにインテリアがきちんと指定されている。きわめてオーソドックスで私には好もしかったので、わずかな小物を付加するだけてスムーズに描けた。壁材からブラインドまでイタリアのものを用い、天然素材を惜気もなく使ったところは、いっそ爽快である。

こうしたせっかくの素材だが、質感の表現は難しすぎて、実物の高級感に及ばない。そこで建物・テラス・戸外の緑と連なる関係を中心に、どれだけ豊かな空間を広げられるか、どれだけ「正調」のゆとりを伝えられるかに重点をおいた。それでいて単調な統一感でつなぐのではなく、どこかでバランスを崩そうとしている。色彩はある程度省略して白で抑えたりしたが、気持ちの上でひさびさに「建築に忠実」を意識してしまった。日本で「ヨーロッパする」という巡りあわせに、いつもの毒気を抜かれたようである。

CASA MIA show houses have been built by the CASA PROJECT Co.,Ltd. on the shore of Lake Kawaguchi and will be open to the public this autumn adopting a very new sales campaign ; with the intention of creating a common basis for comunication and an ongoing discourse, the potential customer is offered the experience of living a day in one of these houses, thereby allowing him easy access to the architect, who, working in the design room located in the site, is always available for consultation.

It felt strange to be working on the illustrations for houses to be built in a purely western style ; there are no tatami rooms. But producing illustrations for houses so thoroughly western also gave me a fresh insight into our lifestyle. Since being involved in this project, I have come to realize, by living in a western style house in Japan, the possibility of understanding its intrinsic nature, and thereby comprehending the advantages and disadvantages of both the western and Japanese forms.

The wall covering and blinds are Italian made, and the natural materials have been freely used. But it is almost impossible to give a true impression of the high quality of these materials on the illustration, so I emphasize the spacious atmosphere surrounding houses and its environment in combination with its "orthdoxy", without using much colors but avoiding monotony.

CASA PROJECT

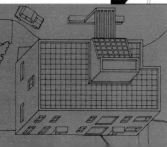

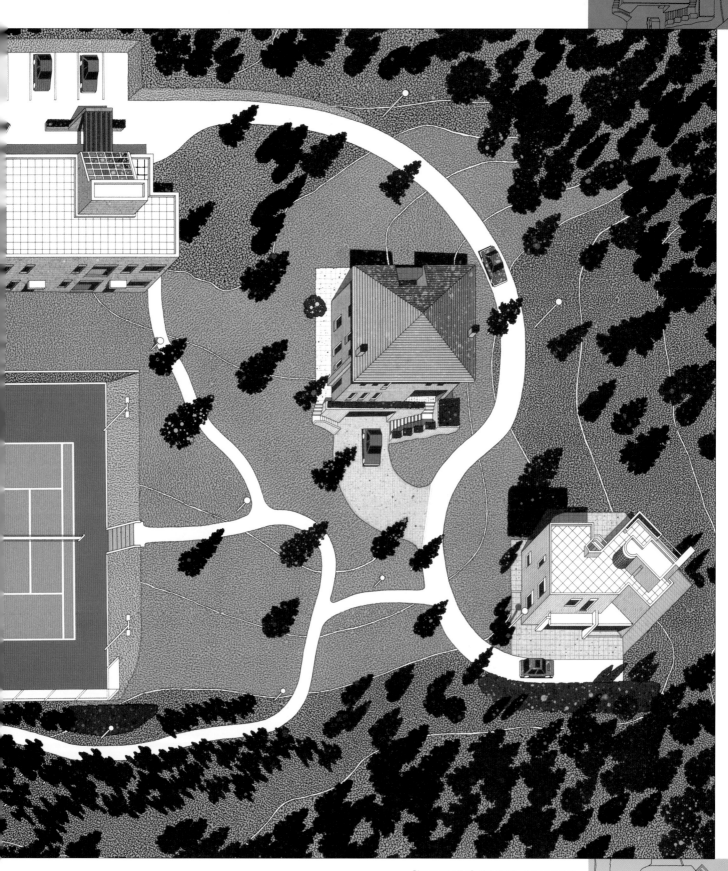

Site plan of ⟨CASA MIA⟩ show houses

CASA PROJECT

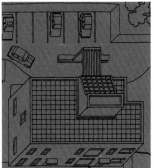

A 〈LIFE DESIGN INSTITUTE〉
B Bedroom
C Office interior
D Entrance

A

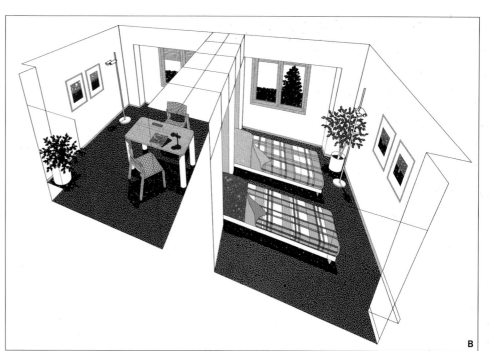

B

C

D

A

CASA PROJECT

A House/B type
B Entrance
C Living room
D Bedroom and terrace

B

C

D

A

B

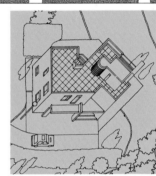

C

A House/A type
B Living/dining room
C Bedroom and terrace

AXIS IS AXIS

アクシス イズ アクシス

1981年にオープンした AXIS ビルは、そのテーマのとおり「デザインのある生活」を求める人々の、名実ともに「座標軸」となった。東京の中のクリエイティヴ・ヴィレッジと称される六本木をはじめとして、デザイン感覚をセールスポイントにした商業ビルはいたるところ無数にあるが、独自のコンセプトを、建物から各店舗の商品構成や情報メディアにまで一筋の乱れもなく貫いている例を、私は他に知らない。

今日、どんな経営体でも「文化の香り溢れる…」といった性格づけを安直に掲げはするものの、その実は文化ならぬ「ただの流行」だったりして、わずか数シーズンでどこにでもある雑居ビル然としてくるところが多い。AXIS の、6 年目を迎えてますます充実した活動を見ても、コンセプトの堅牢さと感性の柔軟さが実証されたといえよう。

カタログやパンフレットのために、何点ものイラストを描いた。幾度となく現場に足を運んで、ワクワクしながら描き進めていった作品だし、私たちの初めての個展を開いた場所なので、今もって思い入れが強い。当時はエアブラシで着彩したのだが、輪郭線のみを残して、あらためてオーバーレイでやってみた。すでに現実に即した情報は必要でなくなっているため、色も適宜変えてみた。案の定、麗しの「AXIS」はまた一皮むけた艶かさで立ち現れた。エアブラシ独特のグラデーションも捨てがたいが、オーバーレイのシャープであざやかで、テクスチャーを超越した表面効果は、やはり今のものである。

このユニークなデザイン拠点は、雑誌『DOMUS』や『NY タイムズ』にも紹介された。自作のイラストレーションも一緒に掲載されたことでもあり、私は公私混同して大いに喜んだものである。

AXIS opened in 1981, and became in name and reality the coordinate axis of design movements. ⟨Living with design⟩ is AXIS's theme. Although Tokyo has a number of shopping complexes, the uniqueness of AXIS is in its consistent and integrated adherence to its original concept of design throughout the building, i.e. the building itself, the shops and their marchandise, and all the design information they produce. AXIS is not about trends, it is about culture.

Although I used to employ the airbrushing technique in many illustrations for AXIS catalogues and pamphlets, more recently, keeping the same process of inking lines, I have turned to overlay films as the color media.

As I expected, through this new media, "my" AXIS reappeared with "her" colors more vibrant and exciting than ever. The fine gradation produced by airbrushing has its own indisputable value, but the sharpness and vividness, as well as the transcending of the texture, produced by the overlay film technique combines a surrealistic punch with a contemporary freshness I am looking for at present. This unique foothold in the design movement was featured in Domus and the New York Times along with my illustration.

AXIS

living / design / concept

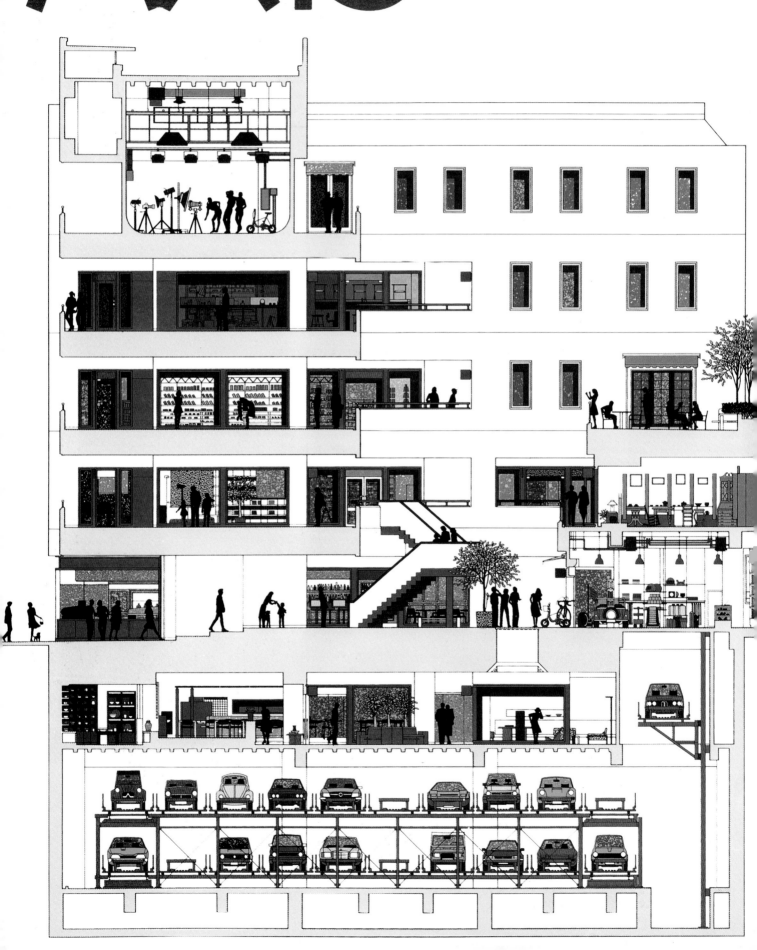

A Poster for AXIS
AXIS shops
B ⟨CHAIRS⟩
C ⟨BUSHY⟩
D ⟨LE GARAGE⟩

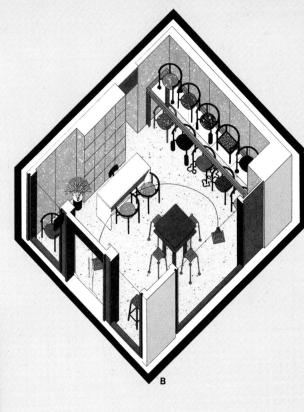

B

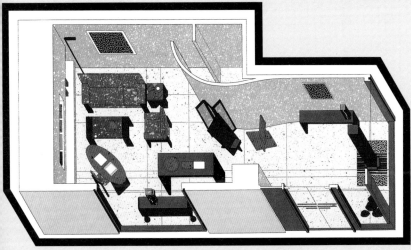

C

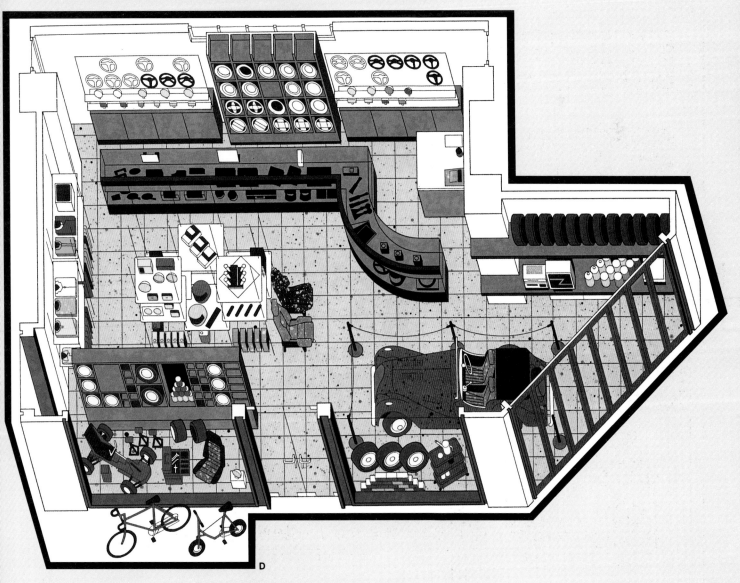

D

AXIS

AXIS shops
A ⟨YAMAGIWA APEX⟩ and ⟨LIVING MOTIF⟩
B ⟨ARFLEX⟩
C ⟨CASSINA⟩

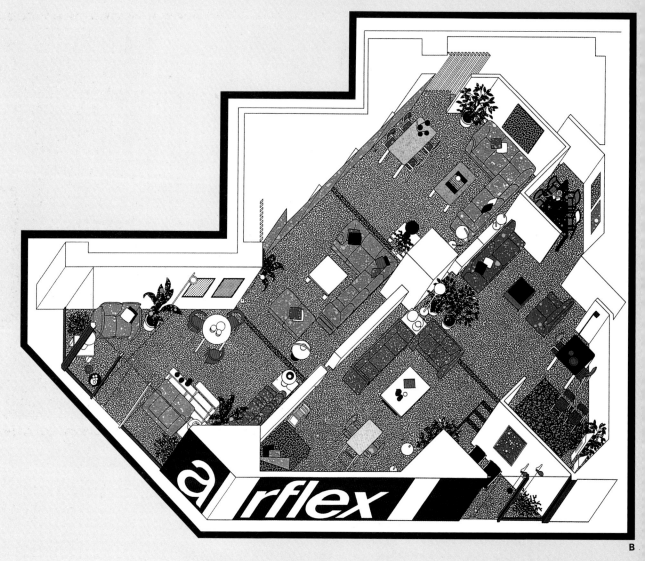

B

A

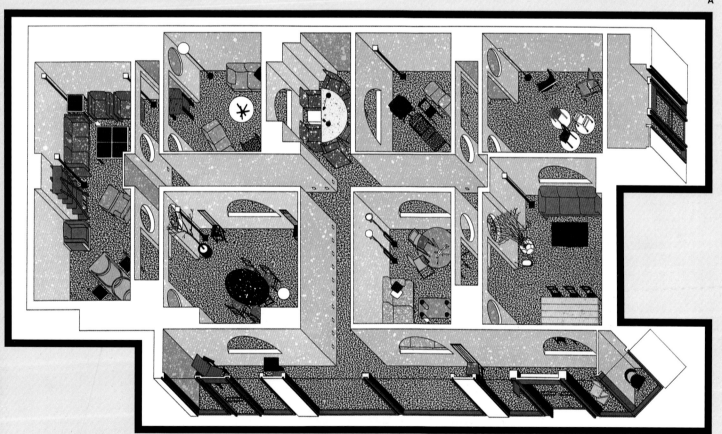

C

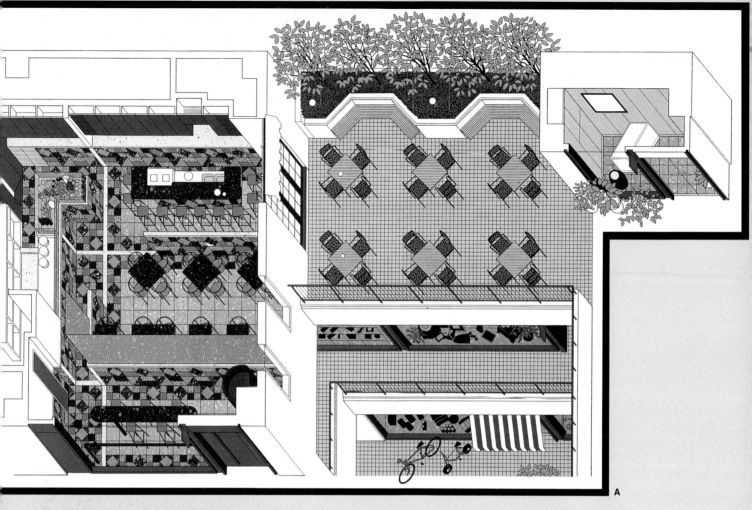

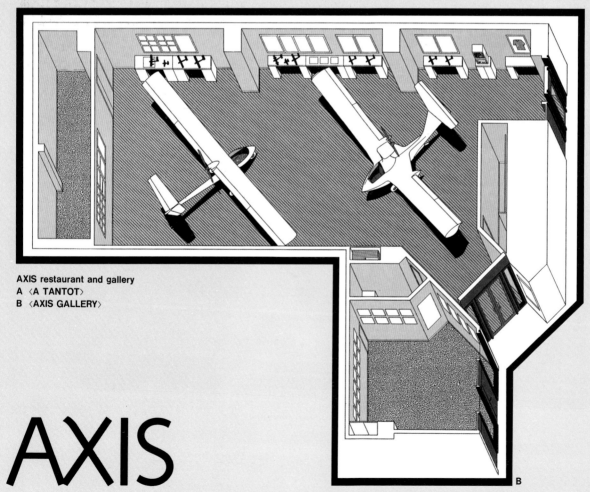

AXIS restaurant and gallery
A 〈A TANTOT〉
B 〈AXIS GALLERY〉

AXIS

AMAZING JAPAN

アメイジング ジャパン

どこでどう結びつくのか判然としないが、「ポストモダン」と「ジャパニズム」は、あい謀ったかのように時を同じくして日本に上陸し、居座ったようである。ポスト風建築を和風レトロで味付けした商業空間が、卑近にして一般的な例だろう。そしてその根底には、我々が洋モノ一辺倒の空間作り・モノ集めに疲れてきた、西洋をかいま見た人々が急激に増えて、真似ごとの統一感を嫌うようになった、という事実がある。逆に言うと、鹿鳴館以来わき目もふらずひた走ってきた路線に疑問をもてるほど、いろいろな意味で余裕が出てきたのだろう。

常に「コンテンポラリーたれ」との至上命令を負ったイラストレーターとしては、新しい動向が認められるや、すぐさまにじり寄るほかない。かつても日本的なモチーフを私はペンやインクで描いたが、あらためて眺めてみると、博物誌に載せてもよいくらい謹厳実直にして侵すべからざるたたずまい、「今」の勢いと軽みにかける。

それをオーバーレイでやってみると、なるほどこれが「ジャパネスク」かと納得が入った気になるから、我ながらおかしい。ものごとを見る人の目は、高められ深められる前に、「新しいか古いか」を見分けるので精一杯であることがよくわかる。成りゆきとか行きがかりで人々の美意識を固めてしまう時代の力、ファッションの強引さには舌を巻くほかない。

絵画にかぎらず、陰影や明暗や奥行を強調する立体感よりも、軽さや平明さや超現実性を内包する平面感覚がうける世の中である。そんなところが、パースペクティヴと無縁の、日本伝統の平面装飾的な表現スタイルを見なおすきっかけになっているのかもしれない。

In Japan, the trends towards ⟨Post-Modernism⟩ and ⟨Japanism⟩ appear to have started simultaneously and have remained. The growth of these trends can be attributed to the recent increase in foreign travel and an awareness that a true aesthetic sense lies not in the emulation and adulation of the western style, but in the movement towards a style that has both its root in Japanese tradition and has embraced the innovativeness of post-modernism. The confidence to reject this previous image of style has come about as a result of this discriminatory ability as well as a general desire to move away from the western style.
When I looked at my drawings on previous Japanese motifs, they seemed somehow outdated; they lacked momentum and levity. Modifying them, using the overlay film technique, brought them back to life.
It is certain that two-dimentional effects which express lightness, flatness and surreality are more popular now than three-dimensional effects which emphasize shading, depth and reality. This could explain why people are looking again at traditional Japanese techniques which tend to be two-dimentional.

■■■■■■

CALENDAR
1987

typical tea-ceremony house

Amazing Japan

caprices based upon Japanese traditional arts and buildings

Illustration: Eiji Mitooka + Don Design Associates

12 December 1986

MON	TUE	WED	THU	FRI	SAT		MON	TUE	WED	THU	FRI	SAT		MON	TUE	WED	THU	FRI	SAT		MON	TUE	WED	THU	FRI	SAT		MON	TUE	WED
1	2	3	4	5	6	7	8	9	10	11	12	13	14	15	16	17	18	19	20	21	22	23	24	25	26	27	28	29	30	31

A Collection of renderings representing traditional Japanese architecture and well-known works of art, following the flight of our imagination.

A Jan/One thousand "torii" to FUSHIMI INARI Shrine
B Feb-Mar/Tiled roofs of traditional houses
C Apr-May/Irises depicted by KORIN OGATA
D Jun-Jul/Stone garden in RYOANJI Temple
E Aug-Sep/Five-storied pagoda in HORYUJI Temple
F Oct-Dec/Noh play 〈KAMO〉

A Stone garden in RYOANJI Temple
B Tiled roofs of traditional houses

B

HOKUSAI's woodcut depicting
behind waves

Five-storied pagoda
in HORYUJI Temple

STUDIES

Study 1/HIMEJI Castle

Study 2/Stone wall surrounding HIMEJI Castle

Study 3/Small courtyard garden in SUMIYA-RYOKAN Inn

Study 4／"Black" drawing room in NISHIHONGANJI Temple

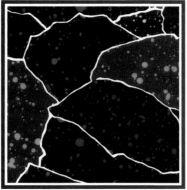

Study 5／CHOSHUKAKU Tea-house

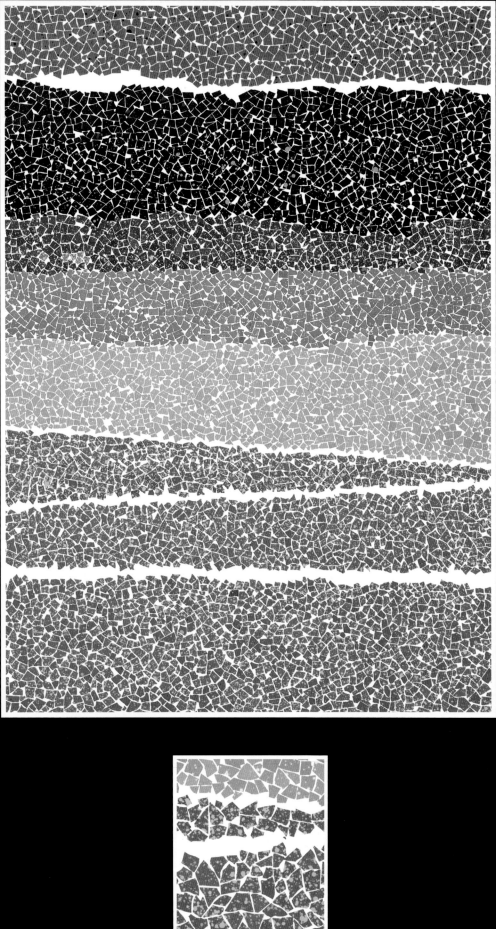

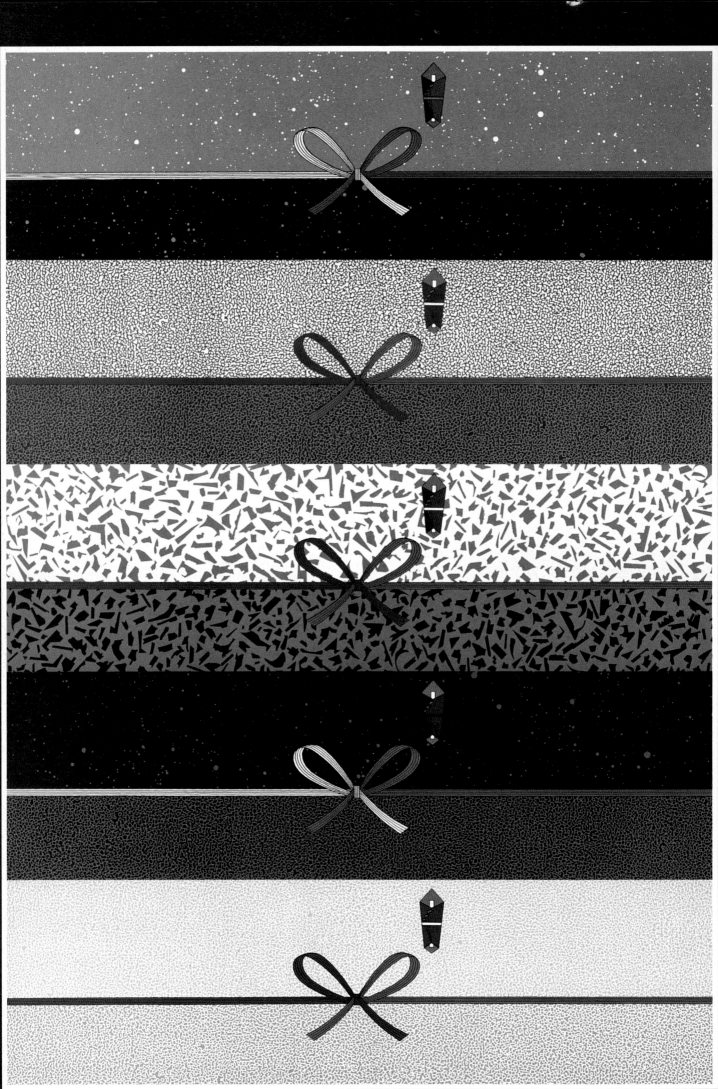

今様

N O S H I G A M I

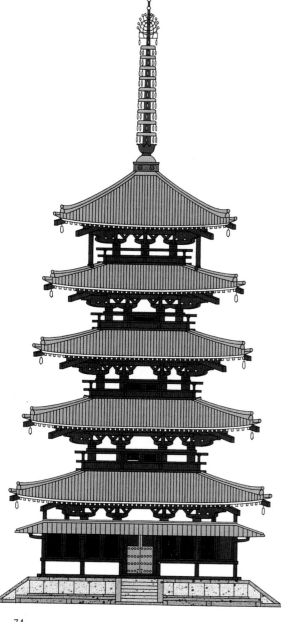

74～76P Cover illustrations for PR magazine／Japanese-style houses

AND ALL THAT JAZZ

その他の作品

「その他いろいろ」を脈絡なく集めた一章である。ここ数年来手がけてきた仕事のなかからジャンルの異なるものを並べた。勝手に作っておいて、これから「仕事」にしようと皮算用している作品もある。建築パースや工業製品のレンダリング風のものがある。純粋のグラフィックがあり、アートディレクションの一貫としてデザインした小物やイラストがある。自分で図面を引いたインテリアや家具やプロダクトデザインがある。企画に加わった施設がある。

こうしてみると雑貨屋の店先のような賑わいだが、おおむね「レンダリング」と「プレゼンテーション」の二つに大別される。前者が質感や機能の表現を重視する「こうなります」の予想図とすれば、後者は「こうあったら楽しいな」の絵といえよう。これはポスターと同じく、印刷されてコマーシャルベースにのったとき一番人目を引くのが使命なので、イメージを伝達し、イメージを増幅させる上で、非常識な色やとんでもないパターンが挿入されている。しかし普通のイラストレーションと違うのは、形やディテールの極端なデフォルメがなく、実物としてのデータが内包されているために、描くことがすなわち設計すること、デザインすることにほかならない点である。

「モノからココロへ」というフレーズがすでに手垢にまみれてしまったように、建物や空間や道具はコケオドシではなく、自分たちが使いこなすものと誰もが思いはじめている。モノに対するマニアックな執着は薄れてきたが、さてモノをどうココロにつなげるかとなると、まだまだ心許ない。両者のスキマからこぼれ出る「落ち穂」を丹念に拾ってゆくことが、今日までの私の仕事になっているような気がする。

Various other examples of my work are presented in this chapter. They include architectural renderings such as houses, housing complexes and industrial products, illustrations of furniture and small articles of my own design, pure graphic art used for calendars, presentations of resort facilities, interior designs, etc.

This wide array of work can, in fact, be roughly divided into two sections ; renderings of products and illustrations for presentations of projects. The former attaches great importance to creating the feel of materials and the function of products. The latter, since its prime task is to attract attention when used in a commercial context, emphasizes the image by using eye–catching techniques such as outrageous colors and unexpected patterns. However the difference between my illustrations and others is that mine basically adhere to the origial design data. So it can be said that my drawing illustrations are equivalent to designing products.

Since the war, we have been voraciously collecting objects with no real understanding of their worth or utility. Today this trend is changing : we have turned back from "things" to "heart", that is from materialism to humanism. But still we lack the complete knowledge to utilize this concept which combines "things" with "heart".

It seems that my work tries to show, through the illustrations, designs and "odd" ideas, how to apply the soft elements of "heart" to our daily life.

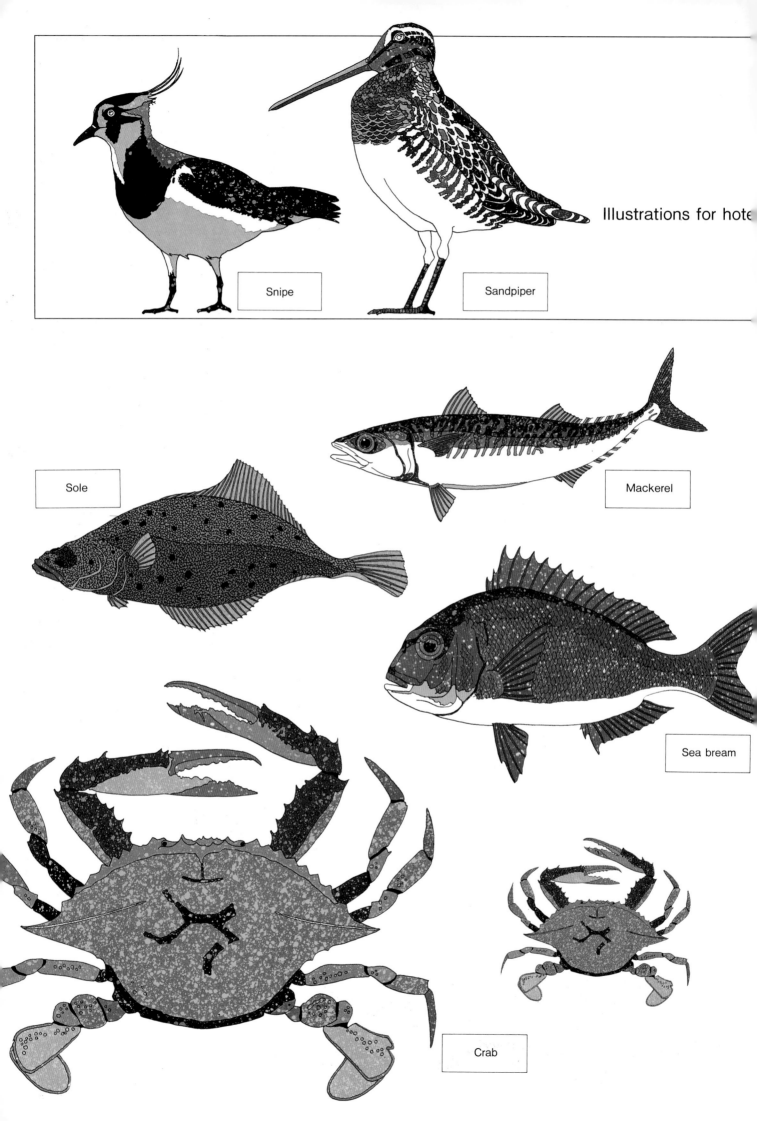

Snipe

Sandpiper

Illustrations for hote

Sole

Mackerel

Sea bream

Crab

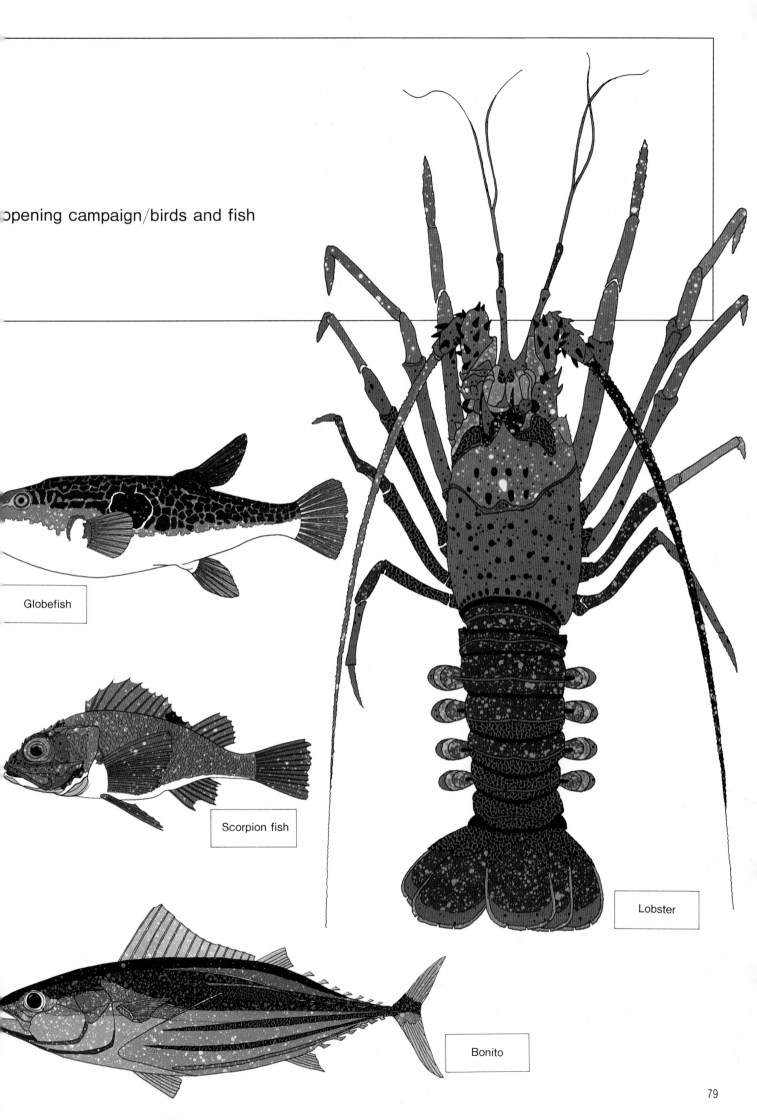

Globefish

Scorpion fish

Lobster

Bonito

P80 乗物／この「キット」は家庭用品メーカーの広告のために作った。毎日の生活の様々な場面を描く宣伝広告にはめこむことが出来るよう，必要な各種のエレメントを集めた。
P81 家庭用品／これら家庭用品の他に，家具，照明器具，食器，人物，植物，動物などがある。社内のグラフィックデザイナーは，それぞれのエレメントを自由に組合せて，統一感のある宣伝活動を展開できる。
P80 Vehicles/This 〈kit〉, created for a company dealing in household goods, has been used successfully in its advertising campaign. Various elements in the above kit were drawn in order to be inserted in advertisements that depict scenes of daily life.
P81 Household goods/In addition to this group of elements, the kit covers furniture, lighting, tableware, human figures, plants and animals. Graphic designers in this company will now be able to develop integrated activities, choosing and combining any of these elements.

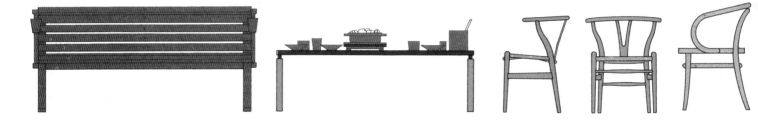

ILLUSTRATION KIT

Furniture and lighting

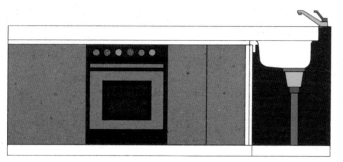

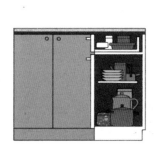

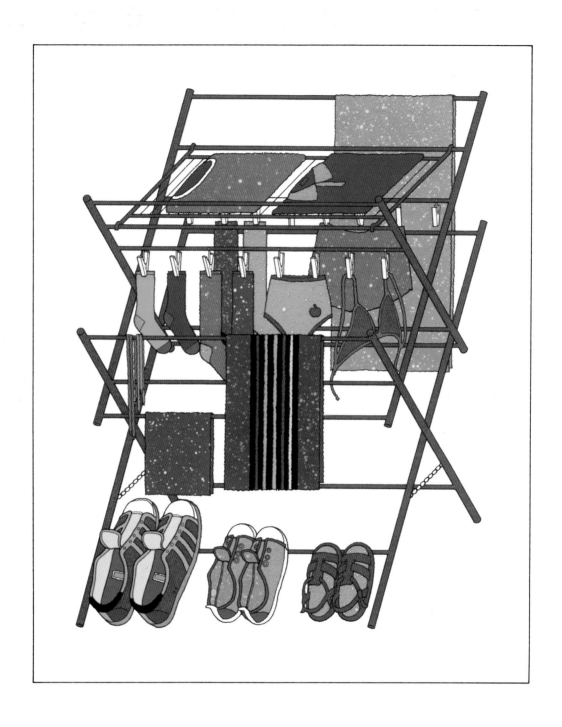

ILLUSTRATION KIT

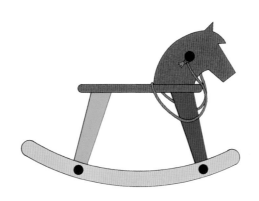

Home living

ILLUSTRATION KIT

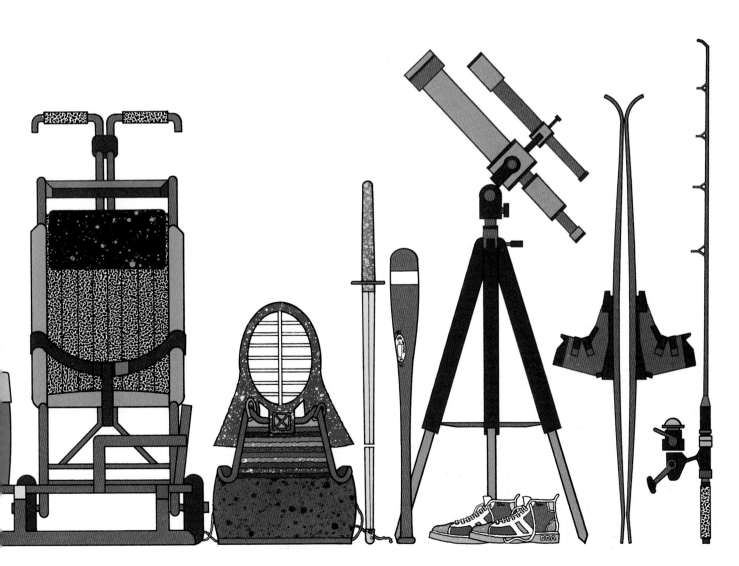

Hobbies and play

Cover illustrations for computer
information magazine/interiors

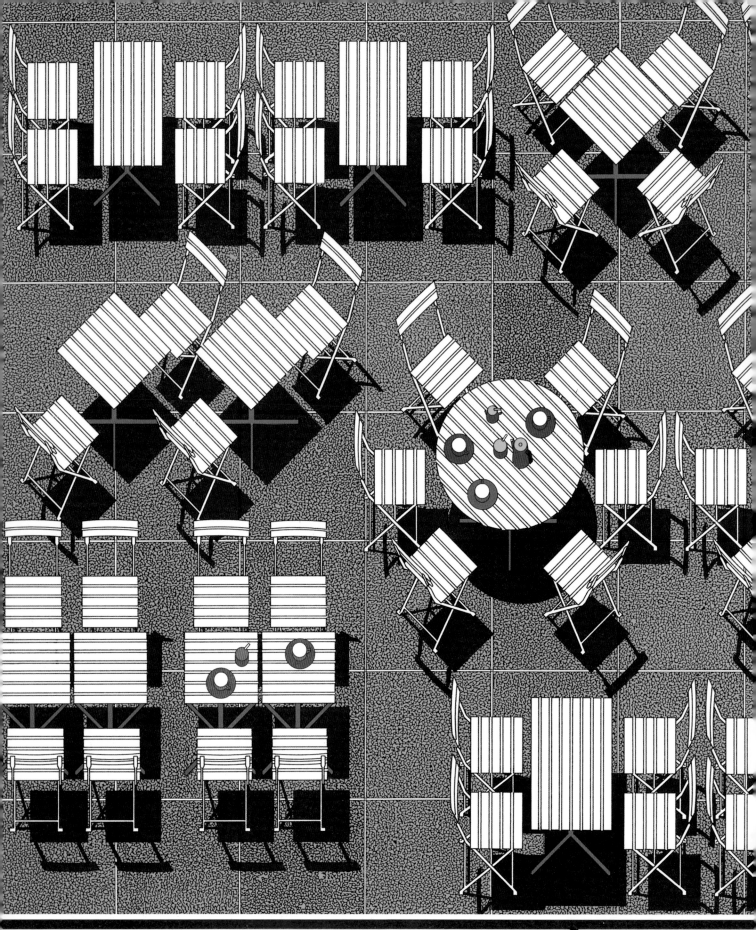

Cover illustrations for PR magazine/Coffee shops

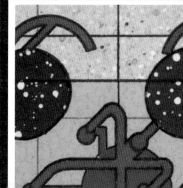

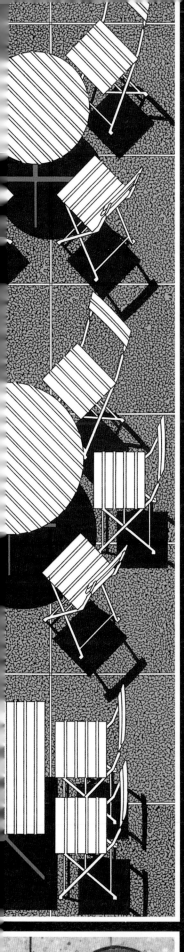

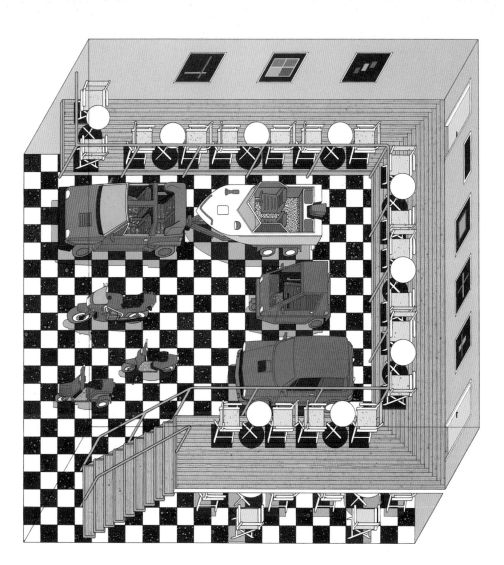

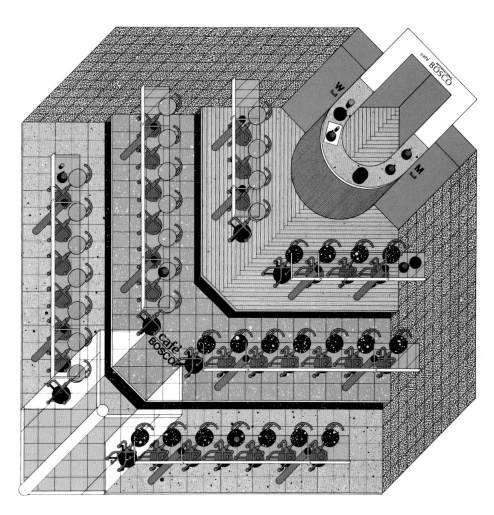

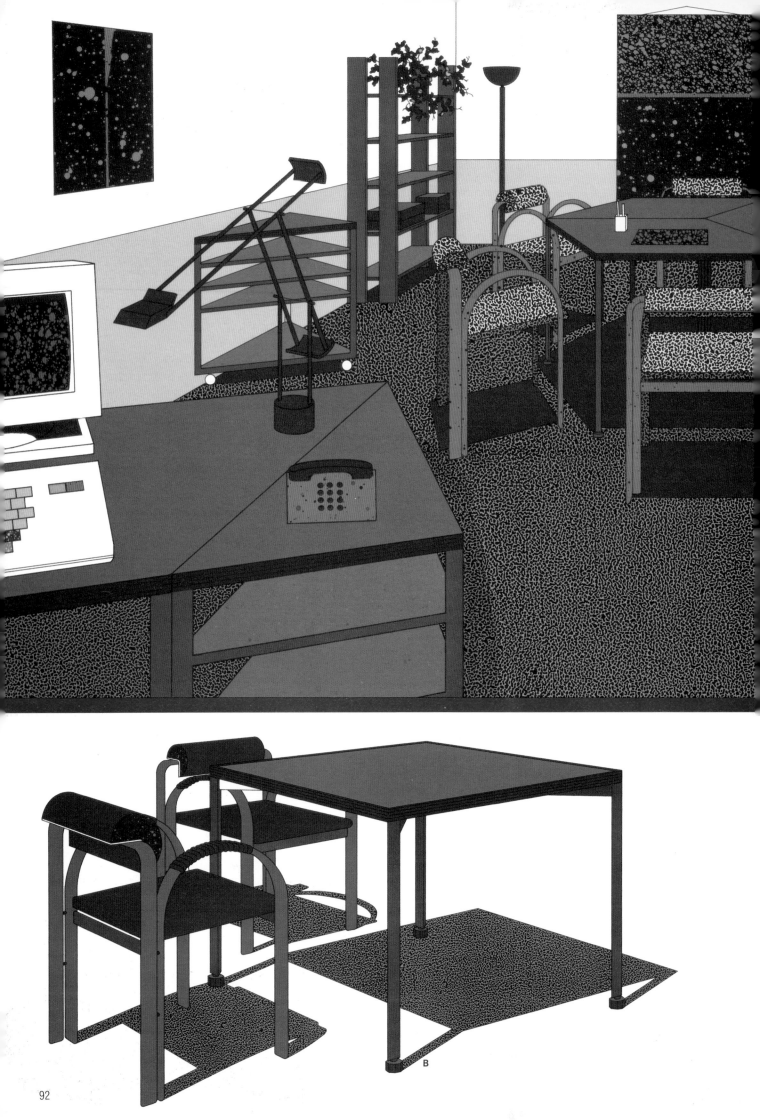

PRODUCT DESIGNS & PRESENTATIONS

A Interior/perspective
B Chairs and table
C Chair
D Rhombic compornent tables

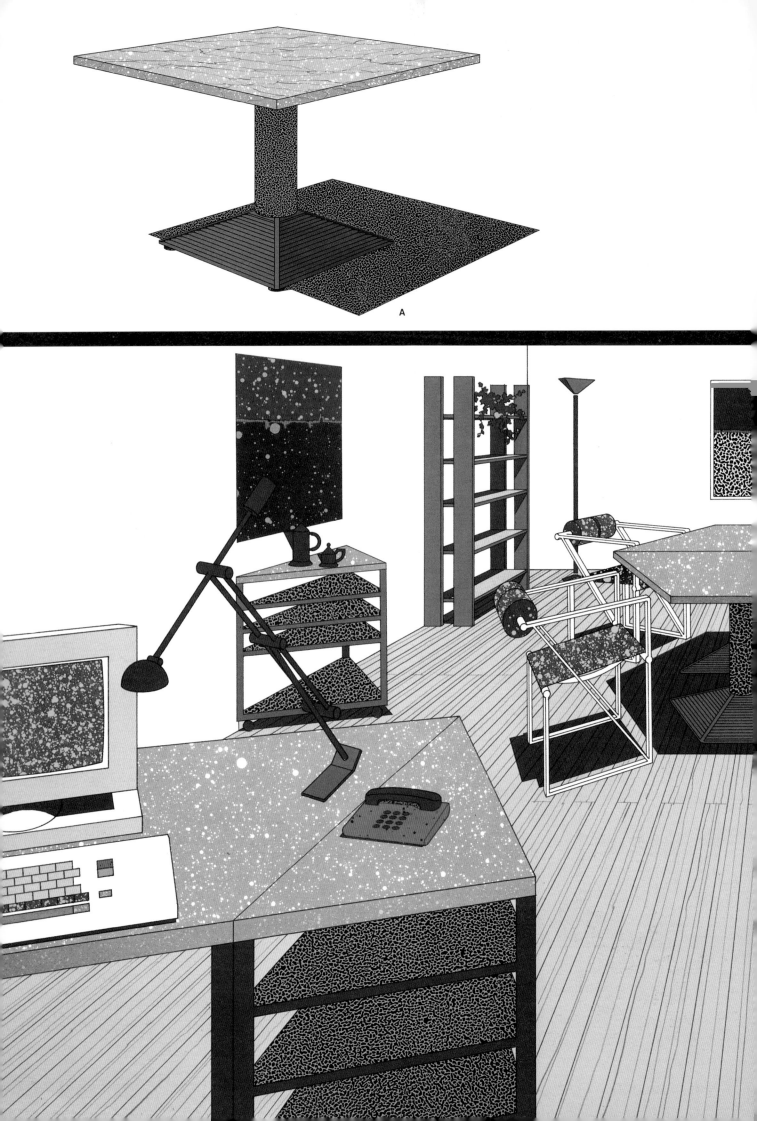

A

PRODUCT DESIGNS & PRESENTATIONS

A Table
B Interior/perspective
C Side tables

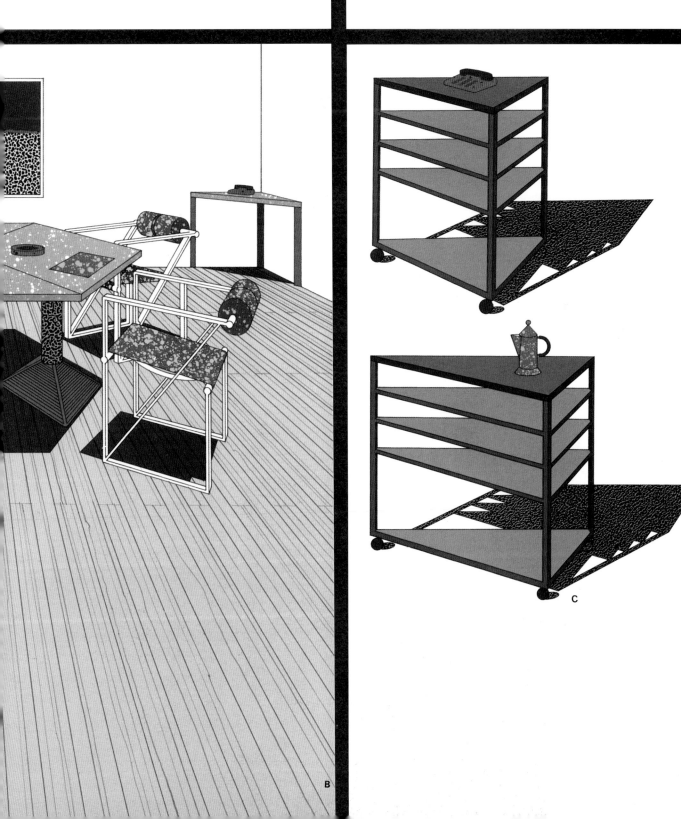

B

C

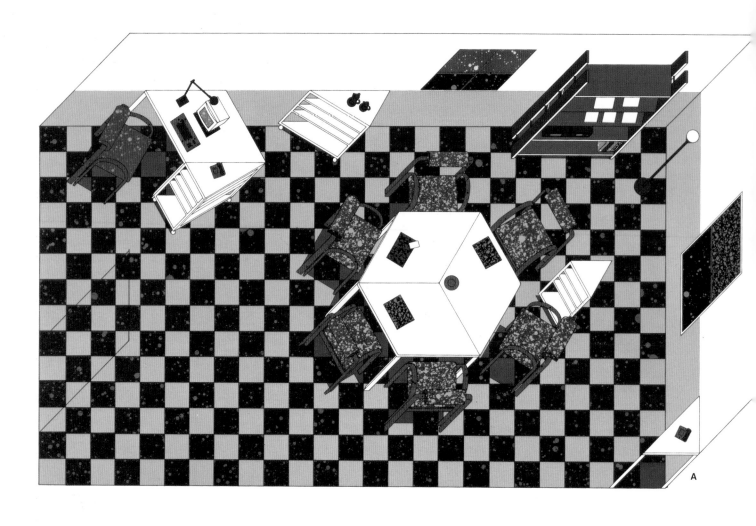

PRODUCT DESIGNS & PRESENTATIONS

A Interior/axonometric
B Shelves

A

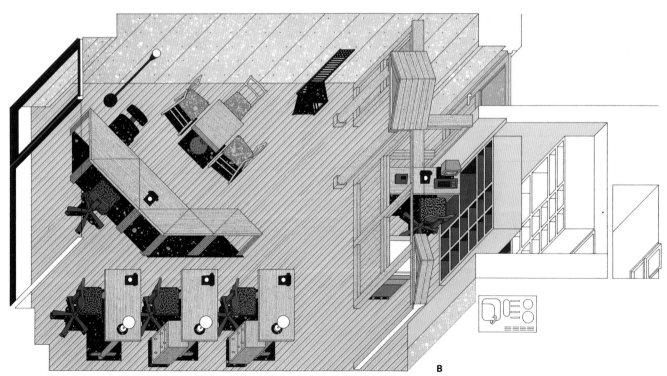

B

A Office interior/perspective
B Office interior/axonometric

97

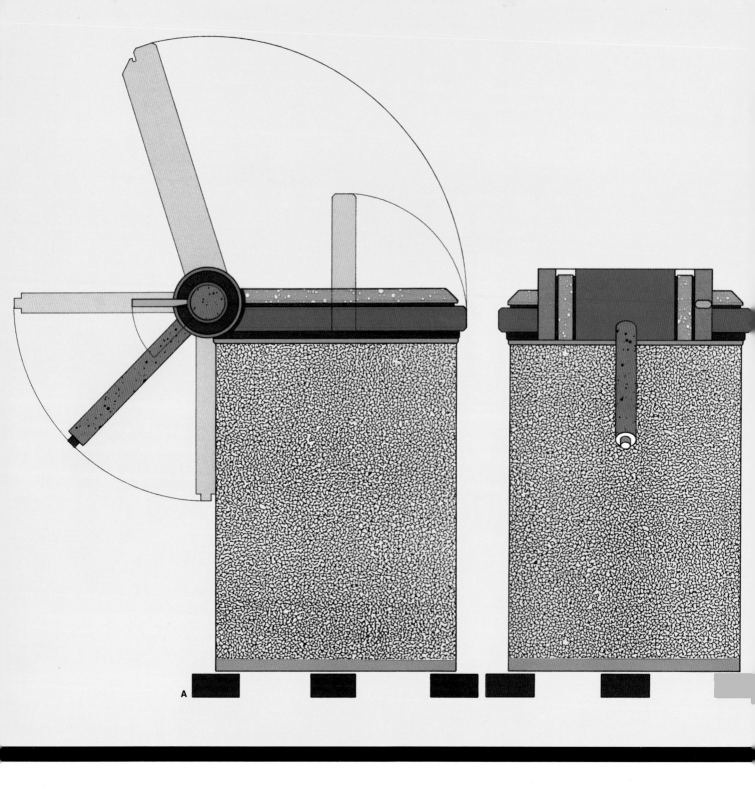

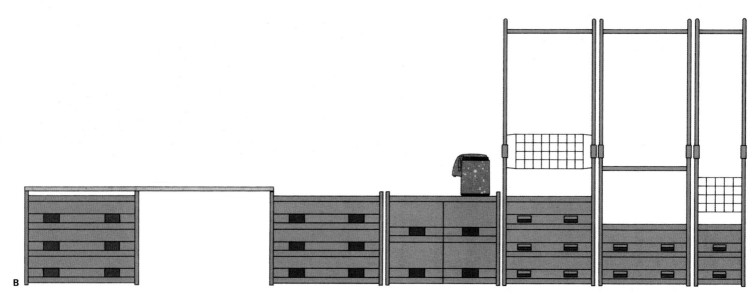

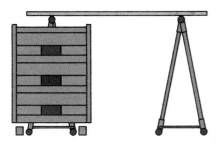

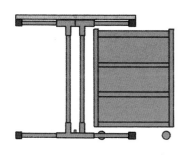

C

PRODUCT DESIGNS & PRESENTATIONS

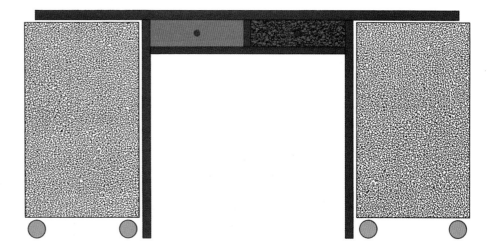

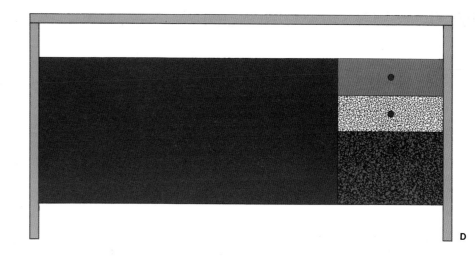

D

A Product design/thermos bottle
B Product design/chests and wardrobe
C Product design/desks
D Product design/desks

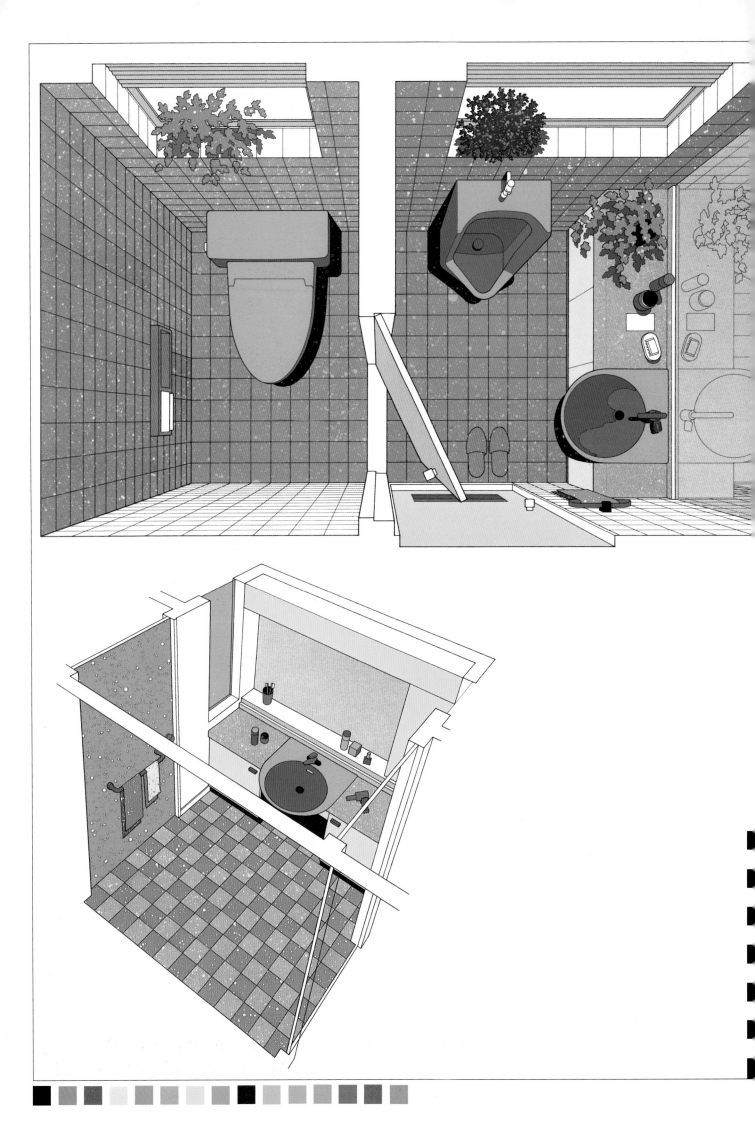

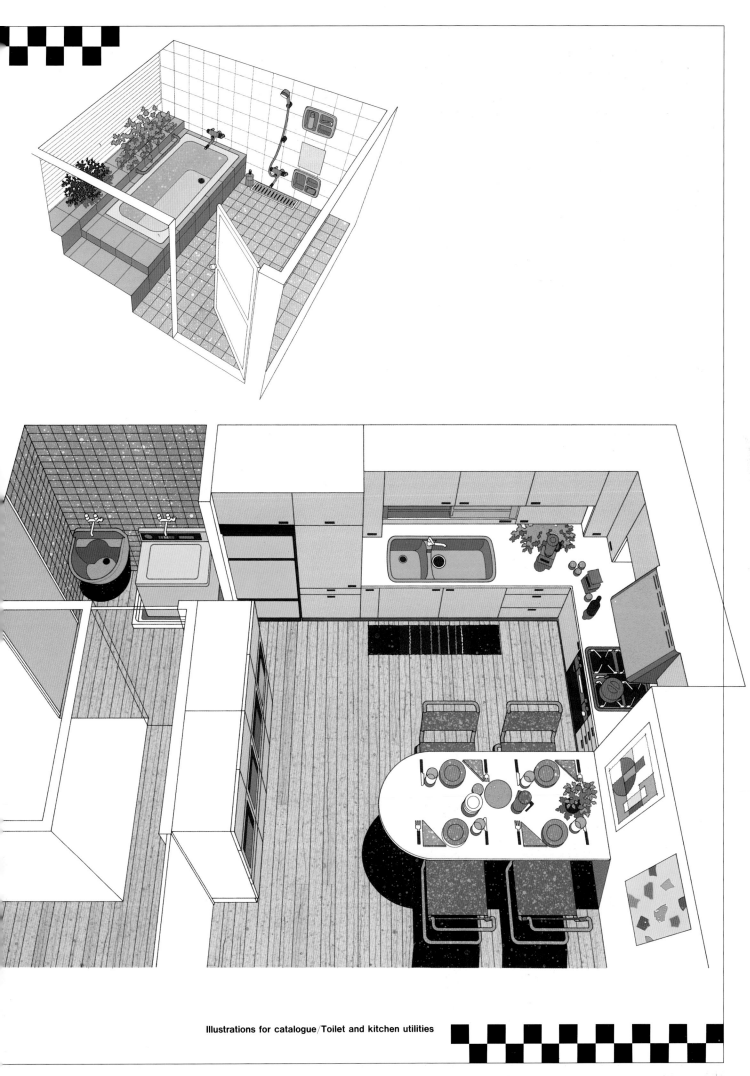

Illustrations for catalogue/Toilet and kitchen utilities

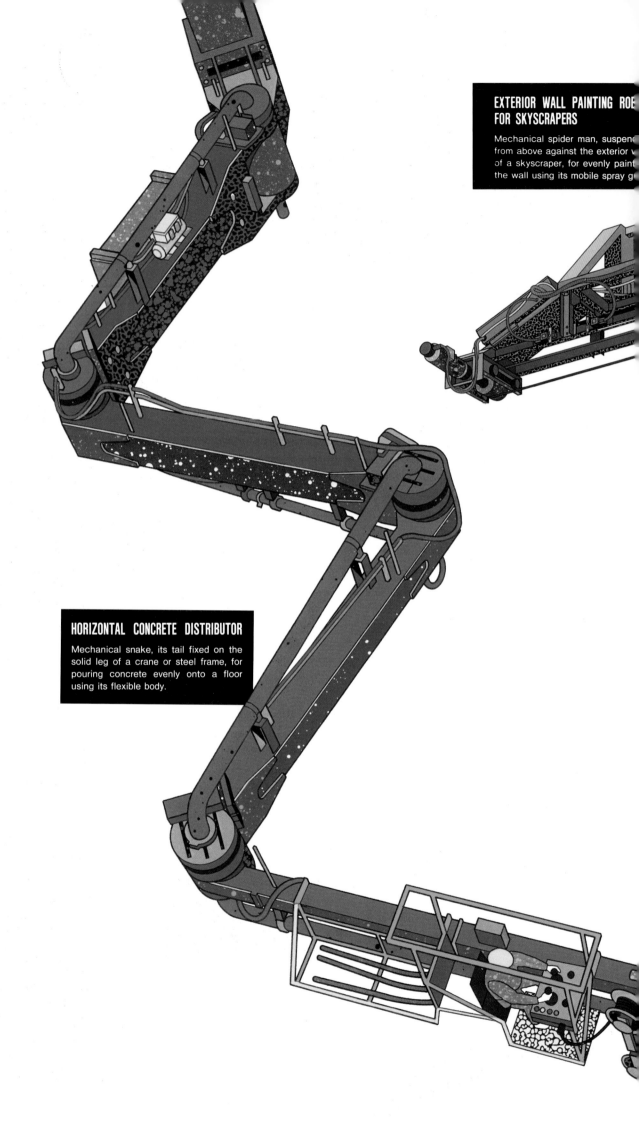

INDUSTRIAL ROBOTS FOR BUILDING CONSTRUCTION

HORIZONTAL CONCRETE DISTRIBUTOR

Mechanical snake, its tail fixed on the
solid leg of a crane or steel frame, for
pouring concrete evenly onto a floor
using its flexible body.

FIRE-RESISTANT COATING ROBOT

Mechanical dinosaur, with a flexible and mobile body, for coating steel frames with a fire-resistant layer using a powerful spray gun; a hazardous job for a man.

CONCRETE FLOOR LEVELING ROBOT

Mechanical horseshoe crab with an automotive body, for leveling concrete floors using a rotating trowel.

ロボットたちの能力には感嘆するが、せっかくの律儀な働きぶりが生かされるデザインとは言いがたい。もっと派手に、もっと可愛く目立つような形と色でもよいのではないか。汚れてもいいような子供服を作るつもりで、ちょっとやり過ぎなくらい遊んでみた。

Considering the amazing ability of these robots, I feel they deserve a better design. I appreciate that being functional and robust are of prime importance for industrial robots, but they could be more colorful and interesting. I went about these illustrations rather as though I were designing childrens' playclothes, using flashy colors and eye-catching patterns to an almost excessive degree.

BEING ABOARD

A

Illustrations for calendar
A Sail cruiser ⟨CANADOS 44X–3/4 TON⟩
B Liner ⟨QUEEN ELIZABETH II⟩

BEING ABOARD
1988

8

MON	TUE	WED	THU	FRI	SAT	SUN	MON	TUE	WED	THU	FRI	SAT	SUN	MON	TUE	WED	THU	FRI	SAT	SUN	MON	TUE	WED	THU	FRI	SAT	SUN	MON	TUE	WED
1	2	3	4	5	6	7	8	9	10	11	12	13	14	15	16	17	18	19	20	21	22	23	24	25	26	27	28	29	30	31

A

747

B

BEING ABOARD

A Helicopter 〈HUGHES 269B MODEL 300〉
B Jumbo jet 〈BOEING 747〉
C Space shuttle 〈NASA COLUMBIA〉

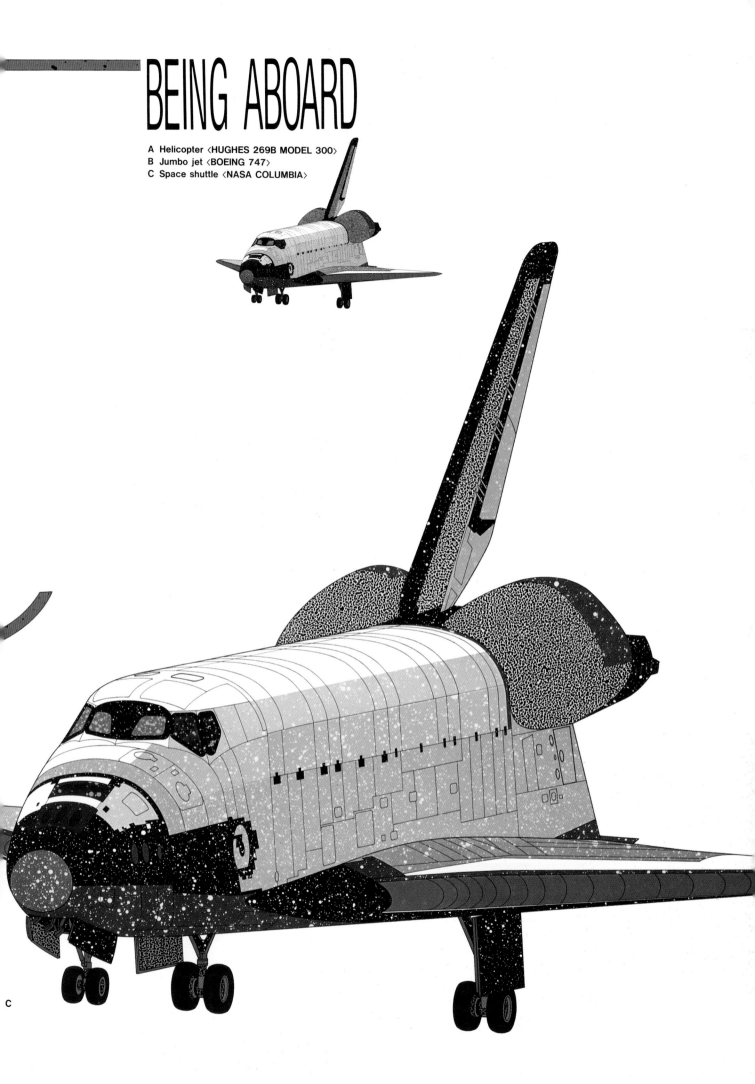

C

DON DESIGN ASSOCIATES

A

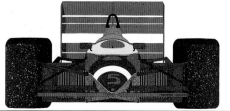

BEING ABOARD

A Racing car 〈FOMULA 1 WILLIAMS HONDA〉
B Sports car 〈MORGAN 4/4〉

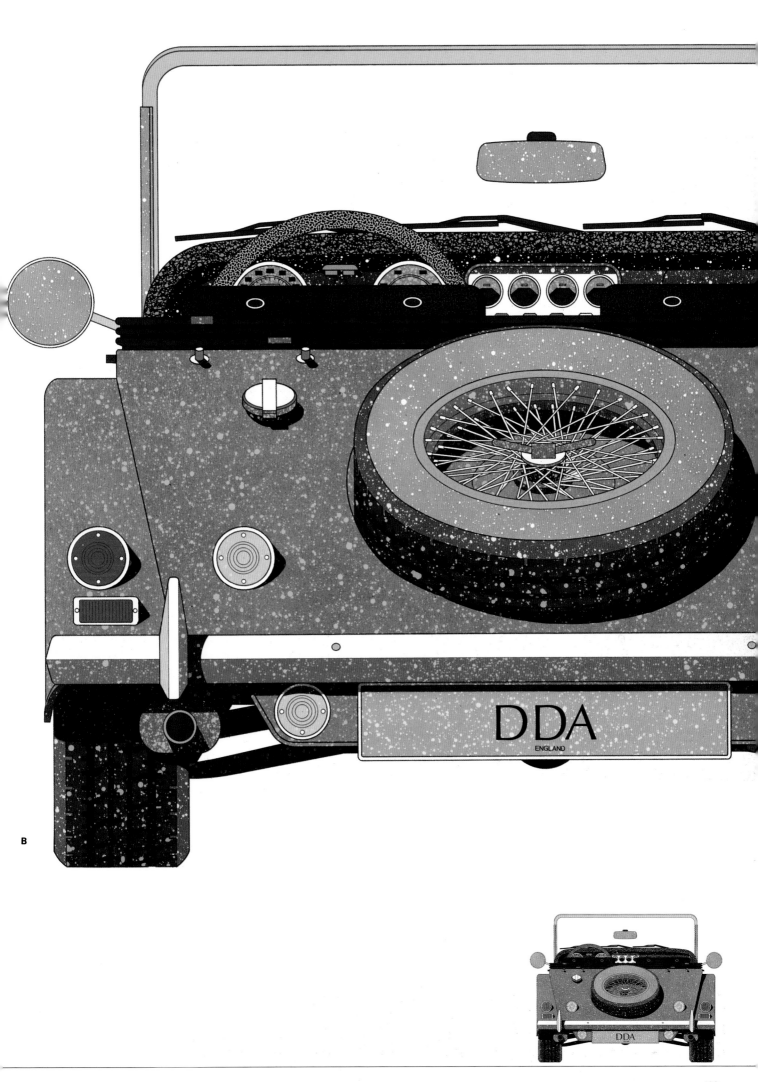

A

B

C

BEING ABOARD

A Steam locomotive 〈C571〉
B Bicycle 〈MOULTON〉
C Sidecar made in China 〈HAPPY〉

CALENDAR 1985

カレンダー〈ハッピーライフ〉1985
「車のある生活」をテーマにしたこのカレンダーは、
大自然の鳥瞰から始まり、湖、森、海、山へ、そ
して車へと視点を近づけてゆく。

Calendar 〈Happy life〉 1985
"The living world of the car" is the theme of
this calendar. It starts with a bird's-eye view
of the natural world, and forcuses in on a
lake, a forest, the sea and mountains. Each
picture features a car.

A House by the sea
B Boathouse and pier
C Cafe terrace

C A L E N D

カレンダー〈光・集い〉1986
12月のクリスマステーブルから始まり、我々の余暇生活への夢を週末の別荘と豊かな環境を舞台に描いてみた。

Calendar 〈Light & Togetherness〉 1986
The cover of this calendar, which starts in December, is an elevation of a family Christmas dinner. The theme is the trend in Japan towards a more leisurely lifestyle depicted by a variety of picturesque weekend houses and their surroundings.

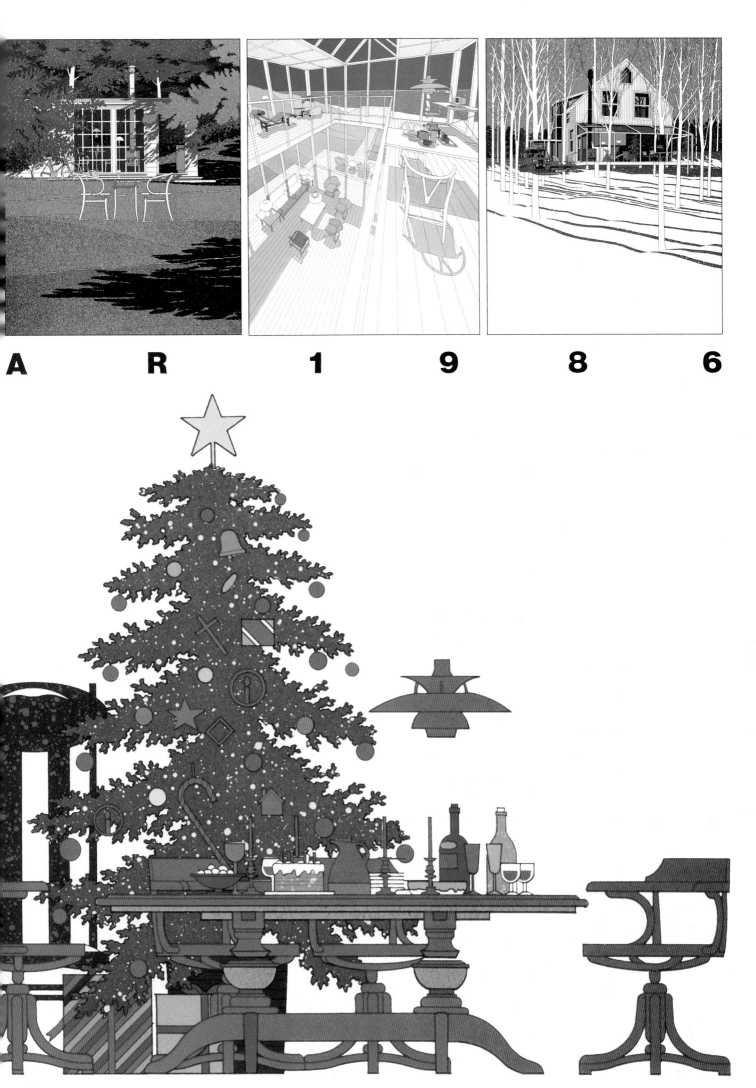

A R 1 9 8 6

7 JULY 1986

Sunday	Monday	Tuesday	Wednesday	Thursday	Friday	Saturday
		1	2	3	4	5
6	7	8	9	10	11	12
13	14	15	16	17	18	19
20	21	22	23	24	25	26
27	28	29	30	31		

8 AUGUST 1986

Sunday	Monday	Tuesday	Wednesday	Thursday	Friday	Saturday
					1	2
3	4	5	6	7	8	9
10	11	12	13	14	15	16
17	18	19	20	21	22	23
24/31	25	26	27	28	29	30

A Afternoon tea in the garden
B Sunny terrace under the trees

House in the winter night

A Living/dining room
B Living/dining room

A Penthouse interior in a hight-rise building
B Computerized 〈Intelligent〉office

ARCHITECTURAL MANUAL FOR CAR SHOW ROOM
IN FOREIGN COUNTRIES

A In front of the show room
B Entrance
C Entering the show room

ARCHITECTURAL MANUAL FOR CAR SHOW ROOM
IN FOREIGN COUNTRIES

A
B

A Front view of the show room
B Display area
C Exterior
D Display area

ARCHITECTURAL MANUAL FOR CAR SHOW ROOM
IN FOREIGN COUNTRIES

A
B

A Front view in the night
B View from the street

SCHOOL

TOWN

PARK

Zoning for safety and comfort/elevation

A

女性雑誌『LEE』の読者の要望をもとに、編集部と住宅メーカーが「本当に住みよい快適な家」のモデルプランを練り上げた。私が担当したのは色彩計画から家具・照明具・小物を含めたトータルインテリアで、編集部とともに、住まいのイメージ作りとイラストの制作を同時に進行させていった。

実際に商品化されたものは多少異なるが、今切実に住まいを考えている世代の人々が企画して、メーカーに「作らせた」試みは画期的である。幸いというか当然というか、売れ行きは好調らしい。

Based on readers comments, after careful consideration, a design for the ideal house was drawn up by the editorial staff of the women's magazine ⟨LEE⟩ in collaboration with a housing construction company. My contribution to the overall design was in providing interior detail i.e. color scheme, furniture, lighting, small articles etc., and while the illustration was in progress, the editorial staff and I were struggling to realize a practical interpretation of their ideas.

Though modifications were made in order that the scheme be commercially viable, this attempt to persuade a housing construction company to build a house, the design of which was based on suggestions from the public, was epoch-making. Fortunately and perhaps not unnaturally these houses have proved to be best-sellers.

LEE'S HOUSE

B

LEE'S HOUSE

A

A ⟨**Main deck**⟩ **that opens into each room**
B **Kitchen and** ⟨**House office**⟩
C ⟨**Lounge**⟩

B

C

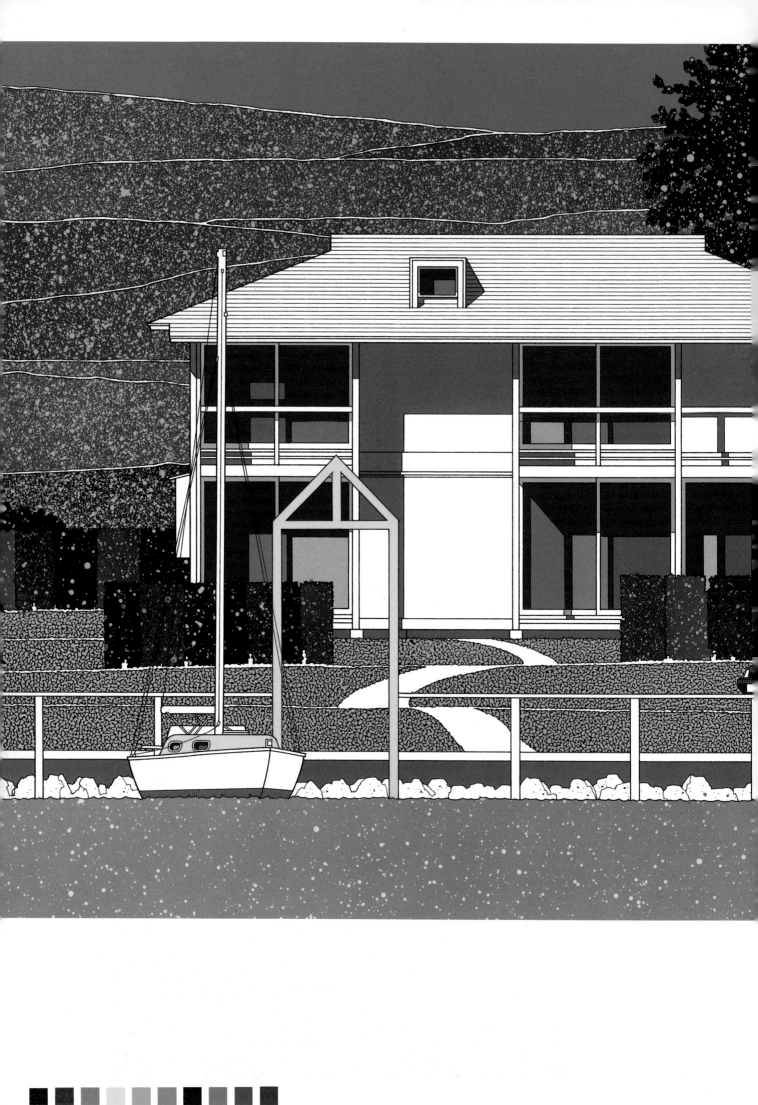

Exteriors of 4 different houses/elevation

Living/dining interiors

Exteriors of 3 different houses

LEISURE RENAISSANCE—
LIVING IN TIME, SPACE, NATURE.
IT'S A REAL NEW CONCEPT OF RESORT LIFE.

A Golf course
B Tennis court/elevation

Interiors of resort condominium
A Lounging by the jacuzzi
B Conference room in condominium
C Living room in condominium

LEISURE RENAISSANCE
LIVING IN TIME, SPACE, NATURE.
IT'S A REAL NEW CONCEPT OF RESORT LIFE.

C
D

A Seminar house
B Interior of hotel/maisonncttc
C Hotel lobby
D Interior of hotel/twin room

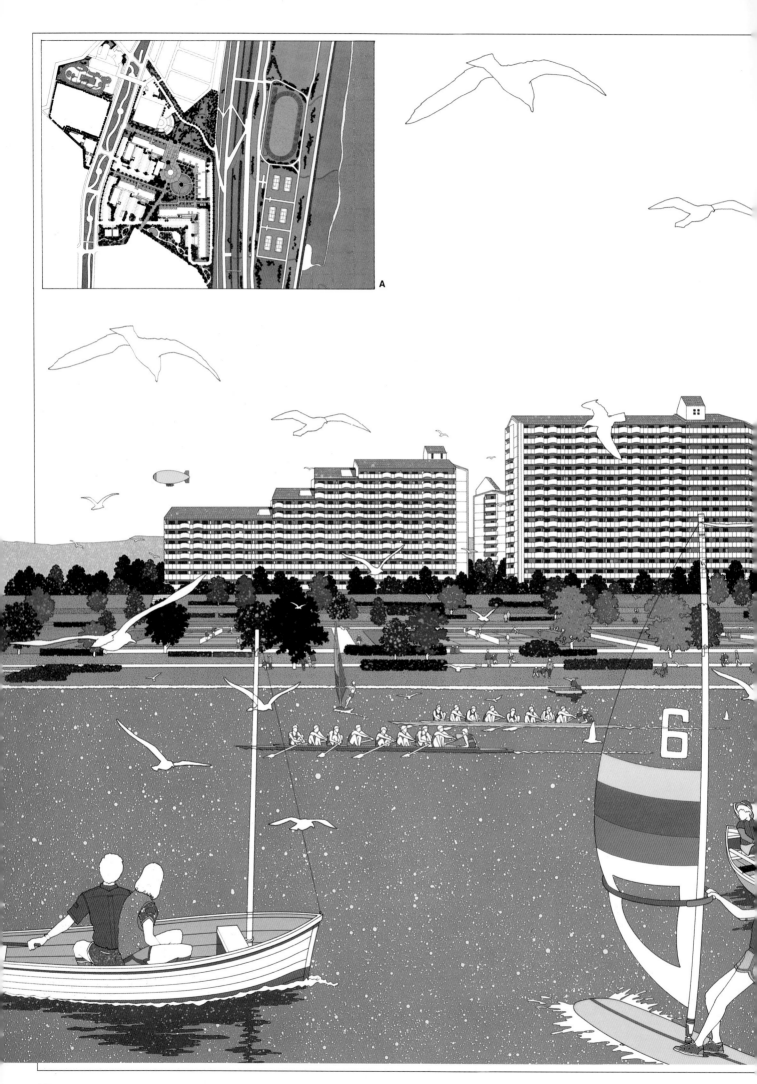

A Site plan of ⟨MAPLE PARK⟩/
  poster, newspaper and other advertising
B Exterior and surroundings
C Bird's-eye view
D Exterior

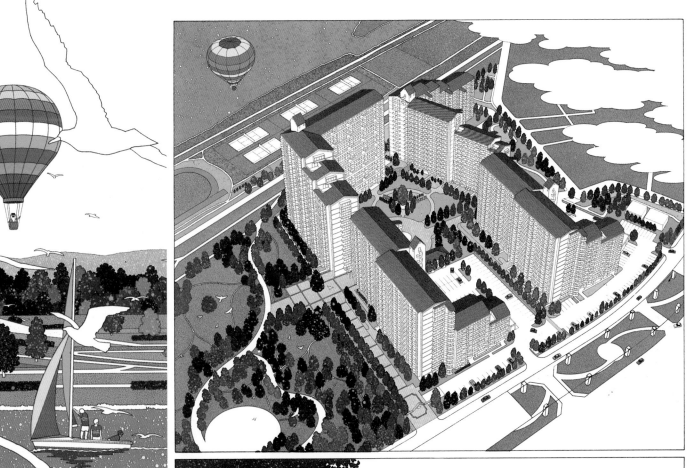

西1番街

B C
D

149

A Elevation of condominium/catalogue
B Exteriors of housing complex/catalogue and newspaper advertising

B

A

A Exterior of housing complex/
  catalogue and newspaper advertising
B Housing complex and boulevard/catalogue
C Housing and footpath/catalogue
D Exterior of condominium/
  catalogue and newspaper advertising

B C D

BASIC TECHNIQUE OF OVERLAY FILM

オーバーレイフィルムの使用法

切り絵、貼り絵が古くから親しまれているように、紙やフィルムを切り貼りして図柄を作り出すという手法は、決して難しいものではない。しかし、私たちのイラストレーションは、墨入れした微細な輪郭線を損なわずに彩色しなければならないため、まず第一に用具の手入れに徹底した注意を払っている。それから先のプロセスは、言葉にすればあっけないほど単純だが、表現効果を上げようとすれば、他の多くの仕事と同様に、目と手によって繰り返し体得するほかない。

The technique of cutting and sticking paper or film to form a picture has long been used in the art of paper cutting and collage. The illustrations used in my work requires coloring without obscuring the extreamly finely inked outlines, therefore keeping the tools always in a perfect condition is of prime importance. Although the basic technique I described here is incredibly simple, perfecting it to express one's own image of the final product, like all other art work, requires repeated practice.

TOOLS

Rotring pen

ボードあるいは厚トレにインキングするにあたっては、常にペン先にゴミがつかないよう注意する。インキングの際には、イラストの性格に合わせペン先の太さを選び、出来るかぎり均一の線を保つようにする。言うまでもないが、描き始めや終りのインクのボタ落ちには気をつけること。ペンは常に垂直に立てて、手もとを見やすくしてスムーズに描く。オーバーレイが付き合わさる部分は、なるべくボードの生地がはみ出ないように太目にインキングする。

When inking over the illustration board, keep the nib free from dust. In order to keep outlines as precise and uniform as possible, select an adequate size for the nib best suited to the character of the illustration. At the starting and finishing points, be careful of accidental dripping of ink from the pen. While drawing, hold the pen upright in order to leave the widest possible surface under the hand. It is suggested that the lines be drawn rather boldly so that the surface of the board will not be exposed between the two adjacent parts of film.

Cutter's knife

カッターナイフの刃は先端のみを用い、上層にあるフィルムだけをカットする。軽いタッチでフィルム上を滑らせるようなつもりで扱うこと。ボードやトレーシングペーパーを傷つけないように、刃先を頻繁に替えることを心がける。カッターナイフには直線用と曲線用があるので、描線によって使い分ける。

Move the cutter's knife smoothly as if it were sliding on the film. Make sure that you change the blade of the knife often. Precision is needed to ensure that only the films are cut. Use two different types of knives——one for straight lines, the other for curved lines.

Pincettes

フイルムを剥がす際に大切な操作は「すくい上げる」ことであり、それには市販のピンセットのままでは役に立たないので、まずピンセットを研摩し、常に鋭利にしておくこと。また、先端が不整合にならないよう注意する。ピンセットは箸をもつように指を添え、フイルムをすくい上げるようにゆっくりと剥がす。

Because the most important process of peeling off the film is to ⟨scoop it up⟩ with the points of the pincettes, the points should be sharpened on an oil stone and adjusted. Hold the pincettes as if holding chopsticks, then peel off the film slowly.

Overlay film

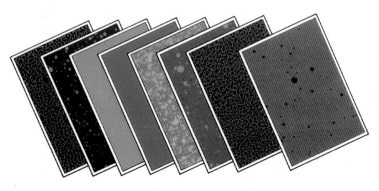

フイルムは塵・ほこり・指紋などが付着しないように、常に清潔に保つ。また、寒暖差のある場所には保管しないこと。粘着性を保つために、画面上に貼ったものを剥がすとき、シンナー等の剥離溶液の使用は避けることが望ましい。フィルムを貼る際は、貼り戻す場合も考えて軽く押さえる程度にし、むやみに力を入れてこすってはいけない。なお、フイルムの色は同色でも微妙に異なるので、購入時には十分注意する。

Keep films clean, especially be careful of dust and fingerprints. Do not store them in a place with a large variation in temperature. When covering the part of the board with the film, do not press it hard with your fingertips, but rather spread it softly and delicately. It is suggested diluted solutions, such as thinner, not be applied while peeling in order to maintain the adhesive power of the films. Keeping in mind that there may be a subtle variation of tone within the same color, to ensure that the films are of uniform hues, check each sheet when purchasing.